ENDORSEMENTS

"If you are a coach, you've probably seen umpteen books on the how to's of coaching. What you may not have seen is the research, the data, the thinking of those who have studied this particular niche and are willing to put all that they have learned....out there....for you to use as the situation demands...this book is a must read."

Beverly L. Kaye - Founder/CEO of Career Systems International and Best Selling Author of *LOVE 'EM or LOSE 'EM: Getting Good People to Stay*

"Changing behavior is one of the hardest things in the world, as anyone who has tried to lose weight, quit worrying, or stop some other problem behavior will tell you. It seems like we ought to be able to decide to change something about ourselves and then just do it – it's simple, isn't it? Ken Nowack tells us, "Yes, it's simple – but not easy." As psychologists and behavioral consultants, he works with individuals and organizations, helping to bring about behavior change to enhance productivity, boost profitability, and promote happiness. He understands human behavior in a way that few people do."

BJ Gallagher - coauthor of *YES Lives in the Land of NO*

"This is a practical guide and does a masterful job of providing a clear framework for behavior change, relevant 360 research and conceptual models as well as useful strategies. Not only does it help consultants learn what to do, it shows them why and how."

Anita Rowe, Ph.D. - Partner, Gardenswartz & Rowe, Co-author, *Emotional Intelligence for Managing Results in a Diverse World*

Envisia Learning Inc.
2208 6th Street
Santa Monica, CA 90405
www.envisialearning.com

ISBN: 978-069-275-051-3

Printed in the United States of America
First Printing: 2016

Envisia Learning®, Momentor®, Talent Accelerator® and Cascade® Performance Coaching are registered trademarks of Envisia Learning, Inc.

From Insight to Improvement: Leveraging 360-Degree Feedback

Kenneth M. Nowack, Ph.D.

PREFACE

I have written this book to help human resources practitioners initiate and sustain successful behavioral change in the employees they work with using 360-degree feedback. I hope that it will provide some useful models, research, and practical tools that you can use to enable your employees to move ahead with their developmental journeys that will include some degree of enhanced self-awareness, skill acquisition and deliberate practice until these new skills become a natural part of your internal employees' behavioral repertoire.

In my previous book, *Clueless: Coaching People Who Just Don't Get It* (Mashihi & Nowack, 2013) we introduced a very powerful model of behavioral change, based on strong theoretical models coming from the leadership, health psychology, and behavioral medicine literatures. The Envisia Learning, Inc. individual behavioral change model contains three stages, which I call *Enlighten, Encourage, and Enable*. Each stage represents a milestone for your employees to move through, and if successful, they will be able to transition from *successful adopters* to *successful maintainers* of new behaviors. I think you will find this individual behavioral change model useful, intuitive, and valuable as you work with your employees along each critical stage from an initial readiness to change to the unconscious competence of the most effective performers in any field.

I will begin the book with an introduction to using 360-degree feedback and then summarize current "Best Practices" based on evidence based answers to key questions relevant to successful interventions.

CONTACTING THE AUTHOR

This book represents an ongoing exploration of how to facilitate successful behavioral change in employees at all levels. I welcome reactions from our readers and although we are not always able to respond to every e-mail, we enjoy hearing from (and learning from) our readers. To reach me via e-mail, please use the following address:

ken@envisialearning.com

Table of Contents

ACKNOWLEDGEMENTS

Jack Welch, the retired CEO of General Motors is often quoted to say *"change before you have to."* I have written this book to help others who help facilitate insight, motivation, and successful behavior change in employees at all levels of the organization.

Whether through observing my "running club" members, raising guide dog puppies for the blind, reflecting on my own coaching experiences or trying to make personal changes in our personal lifestyles we are reminded just how challenging it is to initiate new behaviors and successfully maintain them over time. I hope the evidence-based approach and prescriptive answers in the book will be useful for those involved in roles of helping others change whether you are an internal or external consultant or other human resources practitioner.

PART I:

Envisia Learning Behavior Change Model

> If you don't like something, change it. If you can't change it, change your attitude.
>
> **MAYA ANGELOU**

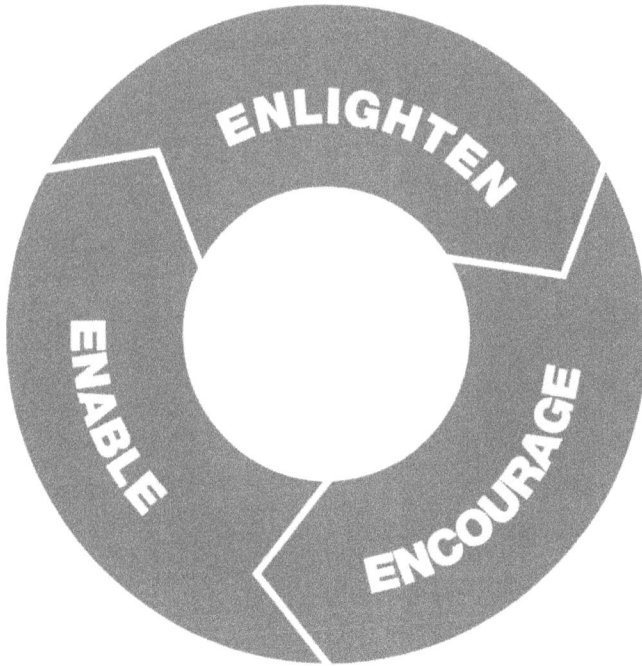

Introduction to the Enlighten, Encourage, and Enable Behavioral Change Model

> Everyone thinks of changing the world, but no one thinks of changing himself.
>
> ## LEO TOLSTOY

Successful behavioral change efforts are often not linear. They tend to be progressive, regressive, or even static. However, to successfully change behavior we all move through *three* specific stages. This chapter will introduce a powerful model for translating the behavioral intentions of your employees into actual implementation goals that can be sustained over time. We call the steps of this individual-based behavioral change model *Enlighten, Encourage, and Enable*. Each will be described briefly below.

ENLIGHTEN

Most people don't wake up in the morning and spontaneously want to change or try new behaviors at work (for example, attempting to listen more effectively, becoming less autocratic, or trying to be more participative and involvement-oriented). Human resources practitioners and leaders must try to get employees to adopt new behaviors and styles that are, at best, awkward and uncomfortable. People only change for a good reason, and becoming enlightened or more self-aware is a necessary but not sufficient condition required to leverage any behavioral change effort. This individual behavioral change stage is characterized as helping employees to perceive, understand, and accept information and data about their thoughts, feelings, and behaviors, either through internal reflection and/or feedback from others.

Insight and awareness are keys to helping your employees understand more about how they are perceived by others, as well as providing the impetus to make behavioral changes that are important to their own health and well-being. For example, learning one has high blood pressure might be the information that prompts a person to learn more about how to control it or that increases one's motivation to change a specific lifestyle habit.

To maintain homeostasis in our bodies, internal and external feedback is the key to correcting and modifying both conscious and unconscious behavioral change. *Feedforward* (Goldsmith, 2002) from others is a great way to help employees learn about the consequences of their behavior and style of leading, communicating, or interacting with others and learn some things they might consider doing more, less, or differently in the future to become more effective. Most human resources practitioners have a large "toolkit" to enhance insight and awareness of their employees. Some useful approaches and techniques for increasing *insight and self-awareness* in your employees include:

- **Utilizing a 360-Degree Feedback Process**. Comparing self-perceptions to those of others are a critical first step to increasing awareness and understanding. Your employees might find value in soliciting feedback from their manager, direct reports, or team members, by using popular, multi-rater feedback assessments that can be done online and will result in a detailed summary report highlighting potential blind spots, as well as strengths.

- **Providing Specific Behavioral Feedback**. Motivation to change can be enhanced when employees are given specific, behavioral feedback in a manner that minimizes defensiveness and denial. Individuals are most likely to change when they believe feedback is constructive and accurate, and when they are helped to identify specific steps they can take to grow and develop.

- **Matching Feedback to an Individual's Self-Insight**. Some Individuals have an accurate appraisal of their strengths and development areas. Others lack true insight about how they are perceived by others. Tailor your feedback to increase motivation by matching your employee's self-insight to your approach in delivering strengths and development opportunities. For example, when employees possess a distortion of "underestimating" their strengths, you might need to help them focus on what they are perceived to be seen as doing frequently and effectively, rather than the tendency to highlight data and information that appears to be negative or critical.

- **Using Self-Monitoring and Reminder Techniques**. We tune into things we try to tune into. Having frequent reminders keeps us focused on our goals and motivates us to move towards completion. Encouraging some employees to keep a daily journal of behaviors, feelings, and thoughts can help build mindfulness and insight about their pattern of response to situations and other people.

ENCOURAGE

There is an old joke that asks: How many consultants does it take to change a light bulb? The answer is: *Only one*, but the light bulb has to really want to change! Employees have to be motivated to change, or any interventions will not result in lasting performance improvements. This behavioral change stage is characterized as moving employees along a readiness to change continuum and building their confidence so they can actually practice new ways to think, feel, and behave. To maximize "readiness" and encouragement, consultants might consider using one or more of the following strategies:

- **Using Motivational Interviewing**. Motivational interviewing (MI) is a useful approach for consultants who work with behavioral change engagements that assist employees in reflecting on and targeting specific performance goals to work on.
- **Assessing Readiness Level**. Identify and determine how "ready" the employee is to initiate new behavioral change.
- **Providing a Change Model**. Introduce employees to one or more of the popular individual, team, or organizational change models in the human resources or mental health professions. This can better help employees understand the typical stages, emotional reactions, and feelings that accompany change.
- **Using Analogies and Telling Stories**. Effective consultants are able to "connect" with others in a manner that motivates and inspires behavioral change. One simple tool and approach that works well to establish rapport and teach others is to tell relevant stories.
- **Find "What's in it for the Employee" To Maximize Motivation to Change.** Integrate the behavioral change efforts with the employee's own career and professional goals and aspirations.

ENABLE

Not all enlightened and truly encouraged employees are successful at changing their styles or specific behaviors. In order for behavioral change to be sustained, employees must know what to change *and* be committed to sustaining it over time. The key to successful long-term behavioral change is the consistent application of a complex set of skills over an extended period of time. This stage is characterized by helping employees track and monitor progress on the implementation of their goals. This includes building a support network at work and home to help prepare for inevitable lapses that are a part of behavioral change efforts, as well as defining rewards for success in actually accomplishing change goals. Some strategies and techniques to facilitate the enablement required for successful behavioral change include:

- **Maximizing Individual Choice**. People are much more likely to grow and develop in areas when they decide which competencies or skills to focus on and when they are capable of setting their own goals. To stretch employees, it is particularly important to maximize choice, whether they focus on behavioral goals or on the type of learning to engage in (e.g., experiential).
- **Breaking Down Learning into Manageable Steps**. When an employee achieves success on specific developmental goals, it paves the way for setting new and more challenging goals. It is important to "stretch" individuals by structuring goals into small, attainable, and manageable steps. Learning and developing competence is maximized when goals are challenging but still realistic and attainable.
- **Using Experiential Techniques**. Reading books, watching videos, listening to audiocasts and attending seminars may be useful, but current research suggests that successful behavioral change can be facilitated much more rapidly and successfully

by using more active group and experiential approaches, such as work sample simulations, case studies, and on-the-job activities (e.g., special projects, stretch assignments, etc.).

- **Building Social Support**. It is well known that we develop best in a social environment where mentors, friends, coworkers, and even family members going through the same change process can help facilitate a person's confidence, hope, and motivation.

- **Providing Relapse Prevention Training**. "Lapses" and "slips" are part of the inevitable journey of personal behavioral change. Understanding what leads to these "lapses" and how to effectively cope with periods of personal stress will enable employees to continue to grow and learn over time, without totally relapsing back to old, entrenched behaviors and styles.

- **Becoming a Professional "Nag" by Using Reminders**. People will often need someone to "remind" them about what is important and not just urgent. Many people have rows of workshop materials and assessments from previous training programs but still have not altered their behavior.

To maximize behavior change success, consultants must use and understand the three key drivers of sustained behavioral change: *enlightenment, encouragement, and enablement*. Consultants who attempt to maximize all *three conditions* will have a much higher probability of seeing a payoff in their employees, than if only one condition exists alone.

Successful behavioral change is not without challenges. Sometimes, the best we can do as consultants is try to help employees become more self-aware and motivated to try new behaviors. After that, a number of social, organizational, and environmental factors play a big role in how well our employees maintain the new behavior until it becomes automatic and part of their natural style and repertoire in dealing with work and non-work situations and challenges. Of course, all employees come with unique personalities, styles, experiences, and genetic set points that also can limit their ability to perceive information, to remain diligent with maintaining goals, and to overcome adversity.

Behavior is never done in a vacuum, and great consultants always consider their work as part of a broader "employee system" that involves the employee's work or home environment, as well as the skills and experiences that the consultant will bring to the intervention. In fact, the best consultants are aware of their own limitations, biases, and experiences that can help or hinder the coaching engagement.

We do know some of the necessary conditions and factors required to ensure learning and lasting behavioral change. In fact, the focus of this book will be on how to leverage each of the three individual change conditions *Enlighten, Encourage, and Enable* to ensure a successful behavior change intervention with any employee.

Factoid: Making Progress on Goals

The most common trigger for a "best day" is any type of perceived progress made at work by an individual or team. A total of 26 project teams comprised of 238 individuals were asked to report daily on their moods, motivations, perceptions of the work environment, what work was accomplished and what events stood out in their mind (nearly 12,000 diary entries). Steps forward (progress) occurred on 76 percent of people's best mood days and setbacks on only 13 percent of those days. Therefore, progress on a job, task or work activity — even a small step many days employees reported being in a good mood (Amabile &Kramer, 2011).

PART II:
Enlighten

The first step toward change is awareness.
The second is acceptance.

NATHANIEL BRANDEN

Chapter 1:
Self-Insight as a Necessary Condition for Successful Behavioral Change

Self-insight appears to be a *fundamental* element and a necessary condition for any successful behavioral change effort. Neural circuits are formed after the repeated practice of new behaviors and we shift from being consciously competent to becoming unconsciously competent (e.g., tying our shoe or driving a car). Self-insight is also one of the major building blocks of emotional intelligence (EI), and lack of self-awareness can result in potential career derailment and strained relationships at work and home (Nowack, 2012; Nowack, 2006).

Research shows that the positive benefits of self-awareness are tremendous. For example, self-awareness has been correlated with both individual and team effectiveness (Jordan & Ashkanasy, 2006). There is also a small, but growing, body of empirical literature supporting the idea that as a leader's capacity for self-awareness improves, others are more likely to rate his or her managerial performance as more effective (Kilburg, 2006). Similarly, a lack of self-awareness is one of the main factors contributing to career "derailment" (Hogan, Hogan, & Kaiser, 2011).

Psychologists studying the effects of an intentional self-awareness technique known as "mindfulness" found that trained participants showed a significant improvement in critical cognitive skills (and performed significantly higher in cognitive tests than a control group) after just four days of training for only 20 minutes each day (Zeidan, Johnson, Diamond, David, Goolkasian, 2010). Additionally, deliberate practice of intentional awareness has been shown to reduce self-defeating thoughts which, in turn, significantly decreased aggressive behavior towards others (Borders, Earleywine, Jojodia, 2010). For example, in a health-oriented study with cancer patients, mindfulness was shown to significantly decrease negative affect, self-reported pain, and stress (Brown & Richard, 2003). Indeed, being aware of our thoughts, emotions, and behaviors appears to be important for our job success, physical health, and psychological well-being.

Awareness/Insight

One of the major goals of executive, life and career coaching is to increase the level of *accurate self-insight*. Unfortunately, just hearing honest and accurate feedback is not enough. True self-insight takes place when employees deeply *understand* and *accept* the feedback. Once feedback has been accepted, employees are more willing to commit to taking specific actions to facilitate personal and professional development.

The *Enlighten* section of the book discusses how feedback creates awareness of an employee's strengths and weaknesses and how they influence different areas of his or her life (e.g. work, family, self, etc.). Particular attention is given to 360-degree or multi-rater feedback systems and their use as useful tools in coaching interventions to facilitate self-insight. When using feedback assessments (e.g., multi-rater or 360-degree feedback) a consultant helps the employee interpret the meaningfulness of the results and explore the differences between self-perceptions and the perceptions of others.

The consultant is also responsible for helping the employee manage his or her emotional reactions to feedback. Feedback reactions may range from pleasant surprise to hurt, anger, and even depression (Eisenberger, Lieberman & Williams, 2003). When feedback is given improperly, negative physiological and emotional reactions are more likely to occur. As a result, harmful feedback can lead to defensiveness, rejection of information, and resistance to using the feedback to improve skills and behavior.

> **Factoid: Meditation and Plasticity of the Brain**
>
> Research at the Massachusetts General Hospital found that practicing meditation on a daily basis throughout a period of eight weeks resulted in a change in brain structure. Magnetic Resonance Imaging (fMRI) tests showed an increase in grey-matter density in areas of the brain that are associated with memory, self-awareness, empathy, and stress (Hölzel, Carmody, Vangel, Congleton, Yerramsetti, Gard, & Lazar, 2011).

Newer neuroscience research sheds light on why negative feedback could be emotionally harmful. Recent studies confirm that emotional hurt and rejection, whether a part of social interactions or a part of poorly designed and delivered feedback interventions, can actually trigger the same neurophysiologic pathways associated with *physical pain* and suffering (Eisenberger, Lieberman, & Williams, 2003). Additionally, interpersonal judgment and social evaluation tends to elicit strong stress reactions, with cortisol levels in our system being elevated *50 percent longer,* when the stressor is interpersonal, versus impersonal (Dickerson & Kemeny, 2004).

When giving feedback, consultants should be aware that its reception will also be influenced by the employee's dispositional tendencies. These should be carefully assessed before engaging in the feedback process. As Joo (2005) has pointed out, feedback orientation and the coach's personality directly affect the employee's openness to the consultant's input, suggestions, and feedback, which can affect the overall effectiveness of an intervention. Research suggests that translating awareness into behavior change may have much to do with how self-aware and ready for change one is to begin with (Nowack, 1999; Nowack & Mashihi, 2012). Such individual differences in reactions to feedback can undermine their effectiveness of setting appropriate goals (Ilies, Judge & Wagner, 2010) for behavior change (Ilies, Judge & Wagner, 2010).

Given the importance of the effects of feedback, consultants need to consider a solid process for facilitating employee awareness. First, consultants should select the appropriate means and tools for assessing employees (e.g., 360-degree feedback, personality/style, etc.). Second, consultants should consider the risks and benefits associated with providing feedback. Finally, they should appropriately cope with employees' reactions. The chapters in the *Enlighten* section will thoroughly explore these issues.

Chapter 2:
Different Domains of Assessment

> Reality is merely an illusion, albeit a very persistent one.
>
> ## ALBERT EINSTEIN

Assessments Used In Employee Development

Depending on their employee's goals, consultants might utilize diverse types of assessments in interventions. It is not uncommon for many consultants to incorporate their favorite assessments to measure specific aspects of personality, style, skills and abilities, and interests and values with their employees. Assessments used in employee development can be conceptualized as being in four distinct domains, each associated with specific individual and organizational outcomes. Assessment domains often used in coaching assignments include:

- Skills and abilities
- Interests and values
- Personality and style
- Health and well-being

HR practitioners might focus on one or more of these assessment domains in working with employees and might utilize a variety of approaches, such as interviews, online assessments, simulations, interactive exercises, assessment centers, and surveys, to collect and analyze employees' strengths and potential development areas. Figure 2-1 summarizes the major assessment domains and describes what they are most associated with.

Figure 2-1

Coaching Assessment Domains and What They Predict

Assessment Domains	What they Predict	Examples
Skills and Abilities	Job Performance Career/Life Success	360-Degree Feedback Cognitive Ability Inbasket Simulations Assessment Centers Work Sample Tests Situational Judgement
Interests and Values	Job Satisfaction Engagement Retention	Interest Inventories Values Card Sorts
Personality And Style	Job Performance Interpersonal Skills Social Relationships Creativity/Innovation Decision Making	Five Factor Personality Inventories (e.g., NEO, Innate) Style Inventories (e.g., DiSC, FIRO-B, MBTI)
Health and Well-Being	Job Burnout Absenteeism Presenteeism Productivity Illness	Maslach Burnout Inventory StressScan (www.getlifehub.com/stress_scan

- **Skills and abilities:** These assessments focus on providing feedback on critical skills, competencies, and abilities (e.g., cognitive ability). These assessments have been commonly used in assessment centers because they emphasize the demonstration of competence and performance in specific skill and ability areas.

Measures of skills and abilities have the strongest predictive validity with future performance. Examples include simulations, cognitive ability tests, performance role-plays, and 360-degree feedback instruments.

When the goal of talent development is to enhance specific skills or an employee's performance, assessments measuring specific abilities can be very useful in helping talent increase awareness and facilitate behavioral change. When employees need to better understand how their behavior impacts others, there are no better types of assessments than those comparing self and others' perceptions in the form of 360-degree feedback measures.

- **Personality and style:** In general, personality measures (both general and specific traits) are typically modest predictors of future performance across all job levels (Judge, Rodell, Klinger, Simon, & Crawford, 2013). The two universal predictors of personality that are most predictive of future performance are conscientiousness and emotional stability (two of the "Big Five" factors).

  Extraversion is highly predictive of performance in jobs or roles that are high in emotional labor (i.e., jobs that depend on high levels of positive interpersonal interactions such as teaching, nursing, etc.). Personality and style tools have been favorites of consultants for many years. Each of us probably has a few that we believe provide talent insight, enabling talent to better understand and manage interpersonal relationships.

  Research suggests that conscientious, extraverted, and emotionally stable individuals tend to be the most motivated and successful in the world of work. Further, agreeable and extraverted people are more likely to get along with others and more likely to express the optimistic and positive emotions conducive to effective interpersonal relations (Judge, Picolo, Kosalka, 2009).

Style-based tools are often used to assess specific coaching areas of concern, including decision making, learning, leadership, conflict, and communication. These are the popular "organizational marriage counseling" tools, used frequently to complement other coaching processes, like interviews.

- **Interests/Values:** Although this is counter-intuitive, interests are actually *weak predictors* of performance and successes unless very specific to job responsibilities. They are strongly associated or correlated with job satisfaction, engagement, and retention, so they are important to measure. Making sure that employees' interests and values are aligned with those of the organization is critical in ensuring employees remain challenged and excited to stay with the organization. There are a number of approaches used to measure interests and values, including card sorts, interest inventories, and other validated career assessments.

- **Health/Well-Being**: One area that has been frequently omitted in the consultants' assessment toolkit is measures of work and life balance, stress, health and resilience. Such issues are common in coaching engagements, and our own research suggests that *40 to 60 percent* of all employees experience a moderately high level of stress on the job (Nowack, 2000; Nowack, 2006; Nowack, 2008).

We recently explored results from our own validated health risk appraisal, which is called *StressScan* to identify what professional working employees reported being stressed about and how that compared to recent findings from the 2014 American Psychological Association (APA) *Stress in America* survey of 3,068 adults. *StressScan* measures 14 psychosocial scales and has been shown to be associated with diverse individual (e.g., job burnout, depression, physical health) and organizational (e.g., absenteeism) outcomes (Nowack, 2009).

The APA survey indicated the majority of American workers were living with moderate-to-high levels of work and life stress. The average reported stress level was 4.9 on a 10-point scale, down from 6.2 in 2007. Twenty-two percent reported they were not doing enough to manage their stress. The top four sources of stress identified in this survey were money (64%), work (60%), family responsibilities (47%) and health concerns (46%).

Our research supports these findings and has implications for consultants in addressing work and life stress and balance issues with their employees. Our stress scale measures self-reported hassles in six distinct areas over a three-month time period including: 1) health issues; 2) work pressure; 3) personal finances; 4) family issues; 5) social obligations; and 6) community or environmental concerns. We analyzed differences by gender across these six scales in a recent sample of 70 women and 79 men working in diverse industries.

In general, women reported significantly higher levels of *overall* work and life stress compared to men. We found only *two of the six stress categories* (financial and family stressors) were rated as *significantly* more challenging by women, compared to their male counterparts, suggesting that women may still perceive that they have two full-time jobs, one at work and the other when they come home.

It's natural to assume that consultants should expect to hear employees share perceptions of some work and family balance challenges and work stressors. It can be argued that helping employees deal more effectively with work and life balance, cope with stress, and build physical health and psychological well-being can be a useful focus in executive, life, career, or health coaching (Palmer, 2003).

Chapter 3:
360-Degree Feedback Systems

Honest criticism is hard to take, particularly from a relative, a friend, an acquaintance, or a stranger.

FRANKLIN B. JONES

The use of multi-rater, or 360-degree, feedback, the process in which managers, direct reports, peers, team members, and customers provide anonymous feedback to others, continues to grow in popularity (Nowack, 2009; Nowack & Mashihi, 2012; Bracken, Rose & Church, in press). Multi-rater feedback systems have proliferated and are being used for diverse purposes and interventions (e.g., executive coaching, performance evaluation, talent management, succession planning, team building, and leadership development). However, what is somewhat atypical is an emphasis on sustaining successful behavioral change over time as a critical outcome of feedback interventions by consultants using these interventions.

The Popularity of 360-Degree Feedback Assessments

Over the last few years, there has been a dramatic increase in the use of 360-degree assessments within most organizations. Why are so many consultants, consultants, and HRD practitioners using these types of assessment tools? What are the reasons that they have gained so much popularity? The wide use and proliferation of these types of 360-degree feedback assessments can be traced to several trends and development such as:

- Online systems that allow data from multiple sources to be easily combined and summarized into feedback reports
- The search for cost-effective alternatives to the administratively complex, yet highly valid, assessment center methodology
- Current organizational process re-engineering, total quality management (TQM) and continuous measurable improvement (CMI) efforts that have emphasized ongoing measurement and improvement of human, technological, and organizational systems
- The increase of career plateauing within all organizations resulting in employees seeking more specific and targeted job-related feedback for on-going professional growth and development
- Professional and career development for talent at all levels

Potential Benefits of 360-Degree Feedback

The primary benefit of 360-degree feedback is that it provides the participant with an opportunity to learn how others perceive him or her, leading to increased self-awareness (Nowack, Hartley & Bradley, 1999). When done well and adhering to "best practices," 360-degree feedback interventions can help increase the understanding of behaviors required to improve both individual and organizational effectiveness and facilitate successful individual and team behavioral change.

Despite the widespread use of multi-rater feedback, consultants still seem to ignore some of the potential issues, challenges, and evidence-based research highlighting the possible risks and dangers of this type of intervention for coaching. The next section will review some of the limitations and potential harm associated with using 360-degree feedback systems.

The Neurobiology of Feedback

"Sticks and stones can break my bones, but words can never hurt me" is a famous anonymous saying we have heard, but what if we were tell you that it is absolutely false. Think about a time when someone you love and admire gave you critical or negative feedback. Did you feel hurt and defensive? Newer neuroscience research sheds interesting light on why some perceived feedback can be emotionally harmful.

It is important to note that we are biologically "wired" to react to perceived harm and danger, and this "fight or flight" response occurs within *one-fifth of a second* before we become consciously aware of it (Rock, 2008). The SCARF model provides *five interpersonal perceptions* and situations that automatically activate our primary threat and reward circuitry eliciting our natural tendency to approach or avoid them:

- **Social Status**: Perceptions of social inequity, rank, or even power can elicit our defensive response, and this is one of the most significant determinants of overall health and longevity, even when we control for income and education. Status, perceived importance, or pecking order can influence both our reward circuitry (dopamine levels) and threat response. For example, even when someone offers to give you feedback, it might evoke a status threat, a desire not to be perceived as less than the other individual and when we are threatened, we might react defensively to minimize the perceived pain of a drop in status in our own minds.

- **Certainty**: Lack of certainty about the future tends to trigger our activating response in the part of the brain called the orbital frontal cortex.

- **Autonomy**: Perceptions of having little or no control have long been associated with increased cortisol, blood pressure, and feelings of helplessness. Individuals who believe that their actions impact future outcomes (internal locus of control) appear to be healthier both physically and psychologically than those who believe that no matter what actions they take, the outcomes are primarily due to luck, fate, or chance.

- **Relatedness**: The perception of someone being a friend or foe immediately elicits a response either toward the individual for further engagement or toward avoidance, sensing potential harm or danger. Our threat circuitry fires immediately when we perceive someone as a foe, as well as our ability to be compassionate, empathetic, and caring toward the other individual.
- **Fairness**: Perceptions of treatment by others, as well as whether decisions at work are perceived to be fair and equitable, strongly influence our primal threat response and even our health. A recent prospective study of 6,442 male British civil servants explored the relationship between perceived justice (supervisory practices) and coronary heart disease (CHD) in these workers. Employees who perceived that their supervisors treated them fairly had 30 percent lower CHD incidents after adjustment for other risk factors (Kivimäki, Ferrie, Brunner, Head, Shipley, Vahtera, & Marmot, 2005).

For over 25 years, researchers have reported that an individual's ability to make decisions about how they work and use their skills is associated with physical illness and psychological distress, with individuals experiencing less job control being more likely to have a poorer health status (Smith, Mustard, & Bondy, 1997; Belkic, et al., 2000).

Feedback May be Harmful to Your Health

Feedback perceived to be hurtful, evaluative or critical might actually be harmful to your health (Nowack, 2014). In a study by Naomi Eisenberger and her colleagues at UCLA (2003), functional magnetic resonance (fMRI) was used to look into the brains of individuals who were involved in a ball-toss video game projected on special goggles while undergoing fMRI was designed to provoke feelings of social isolation and rejection (Eisenberger, Lieberman & Williams, 2003). The imaging technique takes advantage of the magnetic properties of blood to measure brain activity as a function of blood flow where the greater the flow, the greater the neural activity.

While each research participant believes the game of virtual toss ("cyberball") involves two additional participants, it actually engages the subject directly against a computer program. The first game is equitable, but the second round moves into a frustrating game of "keep away" with the participant literally being "left out" and socially rejected. Research participants reported subjectively being "hurt" and being left out from the social interaction simulation they had experienced. The study concluded that when we feel isolated or socially rejected, we experience this feeling in the same part of the brain associated with physical pain (dorsal anterior cingulate cortex).

Subsequent studies by the same research group also found that subjects with higher pro-inflammatory cytokine levels (IL-6) also reported more subjective distress and more brain activity associated with pain during social rejection. Our body produces these cytokines to fend off pain by causing disease-fighting inflammation with accompanying fatigue, fever and sickness behaviors that encourage social withdrawal.

Current findings also suggest that people report higher levels of self-reported pain and have diminished performance on a cognitively demanding task after reliving a past socially painful event than after reliving a ast physically painful event (Chen, Williams, Fitness, & Newton, 2008). Social and emotional pain is real and, apparently, is the physiological equivalent of physical pain. To "have a broken heart" may be a poetic phrase, but it is one that we now know is rooted in a neurobiological reality.

Factoid: The Neurobiology of Pain Relief

In a study of 256 patients with chronic arm pain (rating of at least three on a 10 point scale), 133 were treated with inert sugar pills (once a day for eight weeks) and the other patients were treated with fake acupuncture (twice a week for 6 weeks). 25 percent of the fake acupuncture group experienced side effects, including 19 who felt pain, while 31 percent of the placebo pill group experienced dizziness, restlessness, nausea, dry mouth, and fatigue (Kaptchuk et al., 2006). After 10 weeks, the pill group reported significant decreases in pain (average 1.50 points), and after eight weeks, those receiving fake acupuncture reported a drop of 2.64 points. The fake acupuncture had a greater effect than the placebo sugar pill on self-reported pain. It is all in our head as this study demonstrates the power of our beliefs on our physical health.

DeWall et al., (2010) also conducted experiments that extended this initial research on the neurobiology of emotional and social pain. In the first experiment, individuals took 1000 milligrams of a pain reliever acetaminophen or placebo pill every day and reported their social pain. Those who took acetaminophen showed a *significant decrease* in social pain and hurt feelings. In a second experiment, individuals took acetaminophen or placebo daily for three weeks. At the end of the three-week period, those individuals played the same ball toss computer game designed to elicit social rejection. While playing the game, researchers monitored brain activity with functional magnetic resonance imaging (fMRI). They found that acetaminophen actually reduced neural responses to social rejection in the brain regions associated with the distress of social pain, as well as the emotional component of physical pain (the dorsal anterior cingulate cortex and anterior insula). This study provides further evidence that the physical and social pain centers in the brain rely on some of the same behavior and neural mechanisms.

It is not at all uncommon for employees to experience strong emotional reactions to both the quantitative and qualitative sections of 360-degree feedback reports generated by organizations or vendors selling these assessments (Illgen & Davis, 2000; Kluger & De Nisi, 1998; Wimer & Nowack, 1998). Feedback to others might be purposefully untrue, skewed to be overly critical or flattering, accurate but hurtful or vague, or of limited value for desired behavioral change. Smither and Walker (2004) analyzed the impact of upward feedback ratings, as well as narrative comments, over a one-year period for 176 managers. They found that those who received a small number of unfavorable behaviorally-based comments improved more than other managers, but those who received a large number relative to positive comments *significantly declined* in performance

In one of the most cited social science research studies, Kluger and DeNisi (1998) conducted a meta-analysis that reviewed over 600 published and unpublished analyses on performance feedback (607 effect sizes, 23,633 observations). They found that although there was a significant effect for feedback interventions, *one third of all studies showed performance declines*. The authors speculated that performance feedback sometimes led to an actual decline in performance, because it led to individuals feeling hurt, disengaged and emotionally upset.

People *do* change following feedback, but the *magnitude* of change can sometimes be quite small and practically insignificant. For example, in a review of 24 longitudinal 360-degree feedback studies by Smither (2005), feedback was significantly associated with positive behavioral change but the effect sizes were relatively small (.05 for peers and .15 for supervisors and direct reports). Atwater, Waldman, Atwater, and Cartier (2000) reported that improvement following an upward feedback intervention only resulted for 50 percent of the supervisors who received it. Even a "glass half-full" interpretation of this finding is not something that consultants should be satisfied with as the ultimate goal of feedback is to help translate awareness into successful behavioral change.

Taken together, these findings suggest that with respect to the behavioral change of leaders and others in organizations, "zebras don't easily lose their stripes." Despite the complexity of successfully creating behavioral change, it is important for consultants to understand and accept that *all of us likely have skill and ability "set points" that may provide an upward ceiling to growth and development for many of our employees*. Therefore, consultants should be mindful of the potential risks, emotional harm and negative emotional reactions that can be associated with using 360-degree feedback interventions and keep in mind that in some circumstances, feedback might actually be emotionally hurtful and even harmful to one's health.

What Vendors Won't Tell You: Limitations and Challenges in Using 360-Degree Feedback Systems

Cigarettes in the United States all come with health warning labels. Perhaps vendors should do the same when marketing and selling the 360-degree feedback assessments that are so commonly used by coaches, consultants, and organizational practitioners. These same cautions apply to multi-rater assessments developed "in house" by many organizations using their own competency models. At least five important factors should be considered when using and interpreting 360-degree feedback interventions.

1. Ratings *between* Rater Groups Are Only Modestly Correlated With Each Other

It seems intuitive to expect differences in perspectives between rater groups, such as *direct reports, peers, supervisors, self, and others*. However, research has shown that the ratings *between* individuals are not as highly associated with each other as commonly assumed (Conway & Huffcutt, 1997; Harris & Schaubroeck, 1988; Facteau & Craig, 2001; Woehr, Sheehan, & Bennett, 2005; Nowack, 1997). In general, direct reports tend to emphasize and filter interpersonal and relationship behaviors into subjective ratings, whereas superiors tend to focus more on "bottom-line" results and task-oriented behaviors (Conway, Lombardo, & Sanders, 2001; Nowack, 2002; Porr & Fields, 2006). Research by Oh & Berry (2009) suggests that, at least for leaders, peer reports are more reliable than the ratings of direct reports.

At a practical level, this means that employees might have a difficult time understanding how to interpret observed differences by rater groups and whether to decide to focus their developmental "energy" on managing upward, downward, or laterally in light of these potentially discrepant results. Consultants should help employees understand the meaning of potential differences between rater groups and what actions to take to address these perceptual gaps.

2. Ratings *within* Rater Groups Are Only Modestly Correlated With Each Other

Suppose the employee has three direct reports. Two of them give very high ratings, and one gives a very low rating. How do the coach and employee interpret this? Greguras and Robie (1995) explored within-source variability in a study of 153 managers using 360-degree feedback. Researchers analyzed the number of raters and items required to achieve adequate reliability in practice. These researchers suggested that if a 360-degree feedback assessment has an average of five questions to measure each competency, it would require at least four supervisors, eight peers, and nine direct reports to achieve acceptable levels of reliability (.70 or higher).

Because employees rarely can find that one "all knowing and candid" rater to provide them with specific and useful feedback, the report suggests that having an adequate representation and a larger number of feedback sources is critical to ensuring accurate and reliable data. Given these findings, vendors who do not provide a way for participants to evaluate within-rater agreements may increase the probability that average scores used in reports may be inaccurate or used inappropriately for development purposes.

3. Perceptual Distortions by Participants and Raters Make the Interpretation of 360-Degree Feedback Results Challenging

A triad of positive illusions that we all tend to possess to remain psychologically healthy and that would appear to be important moderators of multi-rater feedback interventions has been previously posited by Taylor & Brown (1988) that would appear to be important moderators of multi-rater feedback interventions:

- People tend to inflate perceptions of their skills and abilities
- People typically exaggerate their perceived control over work and life events
- People generally express unrealistic optimism about the future

The prevalence of self-enhancement is not hotly debated, but there is continued controversy about whether it is essentially *adaptive* or *maladaptive*. This has important implications for understanding and interpreting 360-degree feedback. If self-enhancement is conceptualized as seeing one's self generally *more positively* than others, then the outcomes (performance, health, career, and life success) are frequently more favorable, but if it is defined as having higher self-ratings than the others who provide feedback, then the outcomes are frequently less than favorable (Sedikides & Gregg, 2003; Taylor & Brown, 1988). Consultants should keep in mind that people generally forget negative feedback about themselves, specifically in the areas that matter most to them, and they typically remember performing more desirable behaviors than other raters can later identify (Gosling, John, Craik, & Robins, 1998).

4. Feedback Combined with Structured Follow-Up and Coaching Leads to Better Outcomes

All too often, vendors and practitioners espouse the "diagnose and adios" approach to 360-degree feedback, hoping that self-directed insight alone will result in motivated behavioral change efforts (Nowack, 2007). As previous research suggests, this approach could actually contribute to more negative affect and behavioral disengagement. In one of the few empirical studies recently conducted on the impact of executive coaching, Smither, London, Flautt, Vargas, and Kucine (2003) reported that after receiving 360-degree feedback, managers who worked with a coach were significantly *more likely* to set measurable and specific goals and solicit ideas for improvement, and subsequently they received improved performance ratings.

In addition, Olivero, Bane, and Kopelman (1997) found that feedback and coaching for two months increased productivity over the effects of a managerial training program (80 versus 22.4 percent) for 31 participants. Finally, a recent doctoral dissertation that evaluated the effectiveness of 360-degree feedback interventions on 257 leaders found that over 65 percent expressed a strong interest in an online follow-up tool used to measure progress and facilitate individual behavioral change (Rehbine, 2007). These coaching evaluation studies all emphasize the importance of supportive, coach-driven, follow-up activities to help employees translate insight into deliberate practice.

Chapter 4:
Mirror, Mirror, on the Wall: Matching Feedback to an Individual's Self-Insight

---

> There are three things extremely hard: steel, a diamond, and to know one's self.
>
> ## BENJAMIN FRANKLIN

Often, employees perceive themselves differently from how others experience them. According to much 360-degree feedback research, leaders, in particular, are more likely to have inflated views of their skills and abilities (Nowack, 2009; 1997). We know that this is true for both male and female leaders and it is even more pronounced as leaders move up the corporate hierarchy or have a longer tenure with the organization.

Negative Effects of Misperceptions

Unfortunately, effectiveness on the job tends to decrease as self and other ratings are misaligned (Atwater, Ostroff, Yammarino, and Fleenor, 1998). Other researchers found that managers who rated themselves higher than others had more negative reactions to the feedback process and lower motivation to improve. They were significantly less likely to show improvement when they were reassessed (Brett and Atwater, 2001).

Factoid: Clueless Leaders

A global survey of executives and leaders by Korn Ferry International involving respondents from over 70 countries revealed that only 27 percent of respondents thought their boss was doing the job better than they could! In this survey, 11 percent rated the performance of their current boss as poor, 14 percent rated it as below average, and 23 percent rated it as "average." Forty-two percent did perceive their manager as either performing above average or "excellent".

One aspect of "emotional intelligence" is the accurate perception of one's own skills, strengths, and impact on others. The concept of self-awareness is described as one of the four parts of Daniel Goleman's concept of Emotional Intelligence (EI), which includes four key areas (Cherniss, 2010):

1) Self-Awareness
2) Social Awareness
3) Self-Management
4) Relationship Management

Figure 4-1

The Four Parts of Emotional Intelligence

	Perception	Behavior
Self	Self-Awareness	Self-Management
Others	Social Awareness	Relationship Management

A growing amount of research literature suggests that emotional intelligence and emotional and social competence are *significantly associated* with job performance with positions requiring frequent customer and interpersonal interactions, even when mental ability and personality variables are controlled (Cherniss, 2010). Current research on emotional intelligence suggests that, highly conscientious employees who lack social and emotional intelligence perform significantly more poorly than those high in conscientiousness and emotional intelligence (Nowack, 2012; Nowack 2006).

The highest performing managers and leaders are perceived to have significantly more "emotional and social competence" than other managers. Poor social and emotional intelligence (e.g., over-estimation of strengths relative to other raters) is often a predictor of executive and management "derailment" and failure in one's job.

Using the "Gap" Between Self and Others' Perceptions to Identify Developmental Opportunities

The alignment between self and others' perceptions on a 360-degree feedback assessment can serve as a proxy for insight and self-awareness. In other words, this perceptual gap can serve as a metric and an approximation for self-awareness. It is theoretically possible that both the participants and raters aren't accurate in their perceptions and ratings of skills, personality traits and behaviors.

Whenever a number of raters are in disagreement with an individual's self-perception, the coach's role is to bring the employee closer to reality. Consultants can analyze these misperceptions to find strengths weaknesses, and developmental opportunities. As an example, our Envisia Learning *Emotional Intelligence View 360* (EIV360) includes a process by which the gap between self-ratings and the ratings of others is apparent graphically.

This validated, emotional intelligence 360-degree feedback assessment includes competencies that are shown in four quadrants by each rater category, indicating the extent to which self-ratings are aligned with other ratings. Self-awareness can be categorized in four distinct ways (Figure 4-2):

- Potential Strengths (low self-ratings and high other ratings)
- Confirmed Strengths (high self-ratings and high other ratings)
- Potential Development Areas (high self-ratings and low other ratings)
- Confirmed Development Areas (low self-ratings and low other ratings)

Figure 4-2

High 7 — Potential Strengths / Confirmed Strengths

All Raters Rating

B C
A
D
O
P
Q
J M
F
N K L
E
I
G
H

Low 1 — Confirmed Development Areas / Potential Development Areas

Self Rating (Low 1 — High 7)

Average Scores	Self	All Raters
Confirmed Strengths		
A. Strategic Problem Solving	5.20	5.02
B. Achievement Orientation	5.00	5.20
C. Oral Communication	5.25	4.95
Confirmed Development Areas		
D. Adaptability/Stress Tolerance	4.20	4.66
E. Self-Control	3.60	4.00
F. Building Strategic Relationships	4.67	4.30
G. Conflict Management	4.60	3.87
H. Interpersonal Sensitivity/Empathy	4.20	3.49
I. Listening	4.25	4.11
Potential Development Areas		
J. Self-Development	5.00	4.38
K. Trustworthiness	5.25	4.20
L. Leadership/Influence	5.40	4.15
M. Team/Interpersonal Support	5.20	4.43
N. Collaboration	5.00	4.36
O. Written Communication	5.00	4.77
P. Two-Way Feedback	5.00	4.64
Q. Oral Presentation	5.50	4.76

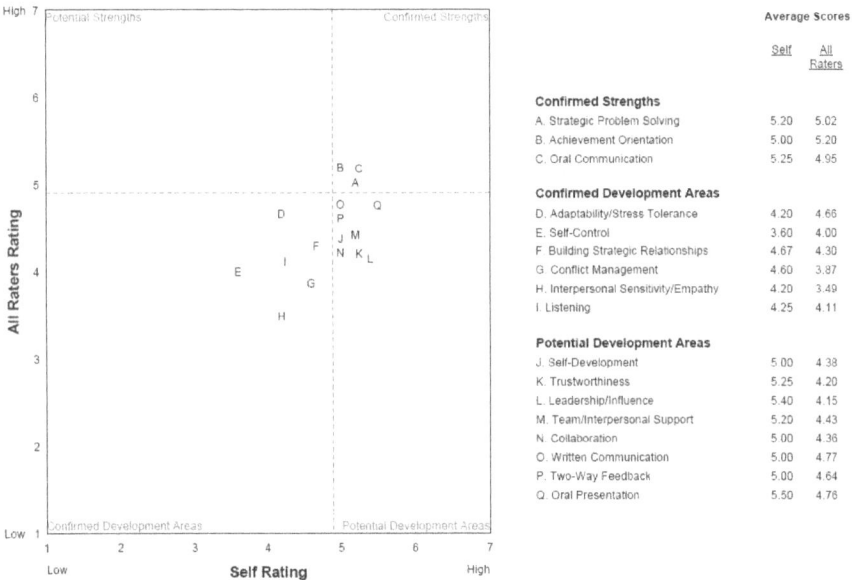

These four quadrants, which are based on the Johari Window (Luft & Ingham, 1955), provide a convenient way to conceptualize a proxy of self-insight by directly comparing self and other ratings on each of the competencies measured in the 360-degree feedback assessment.

Confirmed Strengths vs. Confirmed Development Areas

Confirmed Strengths represent competencies in which the individual's self-ratings are relatively high and matched by how others experience and perceive their behavior. Similarly, *Confirmed Development Areas* represent competencies where both self and others agree that some improvement might be required. An individual with a majority of competencies falling within the quadrants defined as confirmed strengths or development areas might be someone who has relatively high insight and awareness about their behavior. In general, you can expect less defensiveness and challenge in feedback sessions with employees who appear to have a greater congruence between self and other ratings.

Focusing on Confirmed Strengths with Your Employees

Reflect and Manage

Understand and Deploy Your Employee's Strengths: Review the competencies that were rated high and encourage your employee to make a commitment to utilize them on the job.

Combine to Overcome Weaknesses: Explore how combining your employee's strengths can lead to enhanced performance and effectiveness for them.

Explore Team Strengths for Balance: Assess the unique skills and abilities of your employee's team and discuss ways they can utilize these individuals strategically to more effectively accomplish tasks, projects and assignments.

Leverage to Avoid Overuse: Any strength, when overdone, can become a potential liability (e.g., if you are overly analytical you might be seen by others as lacking in decisiveness) so watch the tendency of your employee to overuse their "signature strengths".

| Understand and Deploy Strengths |

| Combine to Overcome Weaknesses |

| Explore Team Strengths for Balance |

| Leverage to Avoid Overuse |

Focusing on Your Confirmed Development Areas with Your Employees

Evaluate Importance and Desire

High Importance/High Desire: In competencies and skills that your employee is motivated to work on and are important on the job, you should discuss ways to develop these further.

Low Importance/Low Desire: In competencies and skills that your employee is not very motivated to work on and are not very important on the job, you should discuss ways to avoid further development.

Low Importance/High Desire: In competencies and skills that your employee is motivated to work on and are not very important on the job, you should discuss ways to explore these further.

High Importance/Low Desire: In competencies and skills that your employee is not very motivated to work and are important on the job, you should discuss the option of refocusing their role or reorganizing work to minimize using these competencies or find others who would be energized deploying these skills to work alongside them.

> ## High Importance / High Desire: Develop

> ## Low Importance / Low Desire: Avoid

> ## Low Importance / High Desire: Explore

> ## High Importance / Low Desire:
> 1) Reshape role
> 2) Find complementary partners

Potential Strengths & Potential Weaknesses

Potential Strengths represent competencies in which the individual's self-ratings are lower than the ratings from other rater groups. Some personality research suggests that these "under-estimators" can be described as highly self-critical, perfectionist, and highly achievement oriented. They may have very high standards for themselves and others and may lack confidence. As a result, these individuals are often less inclined to leverage their strengths and seem to be focused more on their weaknesses or developmental opportunities.

Potential Development Areas represent competencies in which the individual's self-ratings are higher than those of others. Research by Kruger & Dunning (1999) suggests that over-estimation occurs, in part, because people who are unskilled in particular areas reach erroneous conclusions about actual abilities, and this incompetence robs them of the meta-cognitive ability to realize it. In four separate studies, the authors found that participants scoring in the bottom quartile on tests of humor, grammar, and logic grossly overestimated their actual performance and ability. Although their test scores put them in the 12th percentile, they estimated themselves to be in the 62nd.

Interestingly, improving the skills of the participants, thus increasing their meta-cognitive competence, helped the participants recognize the limitations of their abilities. The more skilled that you are, the more practice you have put in, the more experience you have, and the better you can compare yourself to others. On the other hand, the less skilled that you are, the less practice you have put in, and the fewer experiences you have, the worse you are at comparing yourself to others. Over-estimation due to lack of experience is often referred to as the *Dunning-Kruger effect* and may be a possible explanation for these self-other differences in 360-degree feedback assessments.

Additional research suggests that individuals who have an inflated view of their own behaviors, relative to others providing them with feedback, are significantly more likely to experience potential career derailment (Brett & Atwater, 2001). These "overestimators" are likely to display more resistance and defensive reactions to feedback in coaching sessions. Consultants and facilitators can help employees with this overestimator profile to identify strategies to help others better appreciate their skills, efforts and accomplishments. The can also constructively challenge employees about the meaning of these perceived rating differences and how these more critical perceptions might influence relationships and career goals.

Focusing on Your Potential Development Areas with Your Employees

Monitor and Refine

Understand How Others Perceive your Strengths: Review and discuss the competencies your employee rated higher than others. Ask your employee why others might have this impression. Emphasize that even if others have erroneous perceptions, it is important to manage the impressions others have of them.

Refocus Your Branding: Explore developing a new marketing and branding plan for your employee (i.e., how they are seen and the reputation they would like to have). Ask your employee how they would want others to perceive and experience them. Discuss what they can do to help convey a more accurate picture of their strengths and abilities.

Calibrate and Avoid Overusing your Strengths: It is possible that the overuse of your employee's strengths causes others to view these skills and abilities in a critical manner. Discuss how the overuse of strengths can be perceived as a liability to others.

Seek Additional "Feedforward": Encourage your employee to honestly ask others for their thoughts and ideas about how they can continue to excel and improve on the job.

Understand How Others Perceive Your Strengths

Refocus Your Branding

Calibrate and Avoid Overusing Your Strengths

Seek Additional "Feedforward"

Focusing on Your Potential Strengths with Your Employees

Deploy and Evaluate

Identify Need/Opportunity to Deploy Strengths: Your employee's "flaw" is under-estimating what others value and perceive as their strengths. Emphasize with your employee to focus on these and deploy them when they can.

Combine with Other Strengths: Explore how your employee can bundle their strengths to maximize the impact and have a multiplier effect.

Celebrate Success: Research on this underestimator profile suggests that your employee readily sets ambitious goals and are likely to have perfectionistic tendencies. Encourage them to take time to acknowledge and celebrate their successes along the way.

Develop Complimentary Skills: For the areas where your employee might struggle with a weakness, discuss what strengths they possess have which can compensate and help them overcome that particular development area.

Identify Need / Opportunity to Deploy Strengths

Combine with Other Strengths

Celebrate Success

Develop Complimentary Skills

Chapter 5:
Best Practices for 360-Degree Feedback

> I can't change the direction of the wind, but I can adjust my sails to always reach my destination.

JIMMY DEAN

Multi-rater or 360-degree feedback is a critical component of most coaching, training, and talent-development programs. Research on 360-degree feedback suggests some "Best Practices" that, when followed, maximize the use of feedback for future behavioral change. This section will provide suggestions and recommendations for consideration in the implementation of any 360-degree feedback process, based on our own research and practice (Nowack, 2005; 2009).

What is the Purpose of the 360-Degree Feedback Process?

It is important to emphasize that 360-degree feedback is not an end in itself. It is a process to help individuals become more aware of their strengths and potential development areas in order to facilitate behavioral change. It is important to keep in mind that feedback is a necessary, but not sufficient, condition for successful behavioral change. Helping employees understand and accept feedback will be essential in order to enable employees to commit to development goals and actions to enhance their skills and performance on the job. A successful 360-degree feedback intervention involves a series of specific steps that start with why such an intervention should be done and culminate in increased awareness and a commitment to translate this insight into deliberate practice. Let's take a look at the eight steps common to most

360-degree feedback projects (Figure 5-1).

Figure 5-1

The Eight Steps of a Typical 360-Degree Feedback Process

1. Define Purpose
2. Communicate
3. Administer the 360-Degree Feedback Assessment
4. Generate Individual Feedback Report
5. Feedback/Debrief Results
6. Reflection
7. Action Planning
8. Behavior Change

Look at the typical steps illustrated above. What 360-degree feedback does is formalize the natural *feedback* process (Step 1). People observe each other all the time, often unconsciously and unsystematically. They gain impressions, some of which are remembered, and some of which are forgotten. These perceptions are formed continuously in any relationship and result in an impression of an employee's style and effectiveness. The formalization comes from *communication* to the participant and his or her invited raters (Step 2) to think about the participant in a conscious and structured way, usually by completing some form of *360-degree feedback assessment* (Step 3). The data obtained is then processed into a formal feedback *report* (Step 4) containing raters' perceptions expressed in numerical, graphical, and narrative form, which is then presented as *feedback* (Step 5).

The key issue is what an employee will do with the information once they have received it, and that part of the process does not start until Step 6 *(Reflection)*. Reflection involves several activities, including self-analysis by the employee; discussions with a coach, mentor, or supervisor; sharing feedback with others; clarifying things that came.

as a surprise; and validating things the employee is already aware of. Only when this has been done can the employee translate this data into a meaningful and practical *action plan* (Step 7), which will result in successful *behavioral change* (Step 8).

Factoid: Follow Me, I'll make you Miserable

It has been estimated that 65 to 75 percent of employees in any given organization report that the worst aspect of their job is their immediate boss. In fact, estimates of the base rate for managerial incompetence in corporate life range from 30 to 75 percent, with the average level of poor leadership hovering at about 50 percent (Hogan & Kaiser, 2005).

"Best Practices" in Using 360-Degree Feedback: Q&A

This section reviews common questions in the purpose of feedback; the type of assessment or competencies to use; and the implementation, interpretation, and leveraging of 360-degree feedback interventions. Figures 2-5 through 2-8 summarizes these questions in the following categories: 1) The Purpose and Goals of the 360-degree feedback project, 2) Assessment & Competencies, 3) Process an implementation of the 360-degree feedback intervention, and 4) Interpreting the Results and Leveraging the impact of 360-degree interventions. These questions and answers should be helpful for consultants and other users of 360-degree feedback in order to understand and apply some of the latest research and "best practices" to ensure successful interventions.

Figure 5-2

Best Practices in Using 360-Degree Feedback: Q&A
Purpose / Goals

1. What are some of the major features of 360-degree feedback?
2. What is the purpose of doing 360-degree feedback?
3. What are the benefits of doing 360-degree feedback?
4. Does 360-degree feedback do more harm than good?
5. Does 360-degree feedback work (for whom and under what conditions)?
6. Should 360-degree feedback ever be used for performance appraisal or compensation?
7. What if the organizational culture isn't ready for 360-degree feedback?
8. Is 360-degree feedback ever inappropriate?
9. How do you ensure the success of 360-degree feedback?

PURPOSES AND GOALS

1. *What are some of the major features of 360-degree feedback?*

The idea behind 360-degree feedback is to gather information from key stakeholders who can share perceptions and observations about one's skills, abilities, personality, and behavior. This information can be compared to the participant's own self-rating and used for developmental planning purposes. There are many features that describe multi-rater or 360-degree feedback including:

- It typically measures specific behaviors and competencies associated with job performance and success
- It provides a confidential process for obtaining feedback from others who work closely with the individual

- It focuses on observed behaviors that can be modified
- It provides graphical, numerical, and open-ended information to be used for developmental purposes in the form of a summary feedback report
- It provides clarity about one's strengths and insight about potential areas of improvement and development
- It provides a process for improving individual or team performance by continuously providing ongoing feedback when administered over time
- It typically has a development focus without being used for personnel decisions
- Feedback is always anonymous, except for the manager
- Feedback assesses perceptions and not reality
- It is comprehensive and behaviorally focused

2. *What is the purpose of doing 360-degree feedback?*

Feedback in the form of multi-rater systems can be used in a wide variety of human resources systems and interventions ranging from information only to personnel decision making. The most common uses of 360-degree feedback for coaching and development (Nowack, 1999a) include:

- Executive coaching
- Supervisory and management training
- Team building/Team development
- Compensation/Salary increases
- Performance appraisal/evaluation
- Leadership development
- Identification of high potential talent and development
- Training needs assessment
- Talent management and succession planning

- Personnel selection

3. *What are the benefits of 360-degree feedback?*

Since it is not possible to know the one person in the organization who is totally accurate and candid about the perceived knowledge, skills, and abilities of others, 360-degree feedback provides a snapshot of perceptions from various stakeholder perspectives. The use of this intervention can help increase formal and informal communication, open up difficult performance discussions, increase insight and learning, encourage targeted goal setting, highlight specific skills and competencies associated with job performance, and improve performance and productivity. Some additional benefits and advantages of 360-degree feedback include:

- Providing the participant with an opportunity to learn how others perceive them, leading to increased self-awareness
- Encouraging self-development
- Helping increase understanding of the behaviors required to improve both individual and organizational effectiveness
- Promoting an open culture where giving and receiving feedback is an accepted norm
- Increasing communication within an organization
- Clarifying supervisory and managerial expectations
- Being a powerful initiator for individual and team change

4. *Does 360-degree feedback do more harm than good?*

In general, poorly designed 360-degree feedback assessments and interventions can increase disengagement and contribute to poor individual and team performance (Nowack & Mashihi, 2012; Illgen & Davis, 2000; Kluger & De Nisi, 1998). In one commonly cited meta-analysis on performance feedback (607 effect sizes, 23,663 observations), Kluger and DeNisi (1996) found that although there was a significant effect across all studies for feedback interventions (d=.41), performance actually declined in one-third of all studies analyzed for various reasons such as depth of the feedback process, how feedback was delivered, and personality of the recipient.

Several studies have also shown that individuals can experience strong discouragement and frustration when 360-degree feedback is not as positive as they expected (Atwater & Brett, 2005). Brett and Atwater (2001) found that managers who rated themselves higher than others (overestimators) reported significantly more negative reactions to the 360-degree feedback process. They noted specifically that "negative feedback (i.e., ratings that were low or that were lower than expected) was not seen as accurate or useful, and it did not result in enlightenment or awareness but rather in negative reactions such as anger and discouragement" (p. 938).

Newer neuroscience research sheds some interesting light on why negative feedback is potentially emotionally harmful. In general, stressors that induce greater social-evaluative threat elicit significantly larger cortisol and ambulatory blood pressure responses (Dickerson & Kemeny, 2004; Lehman & Conley, 2010). Recent studies confirm that emotional hurt and rejection, whether part of social interactions or poorly designed and delivered feedback interventions, can actually trigger the same neurophysiologic pathways associated with physical pain and suffering (Eisenberger, Lieberman, & Williams, 2003).

In two follow-up studies by DeWall, et al., (2010), functional magnetic resonance imaging was used to test whether a physical pain suppressant reduced behavioral and neural responses to social rejection. Their two studies confirmed that acetaminophen, relative to a placebo control, significantly reduced behavioral and neural responses associated with the pain of social rejection providing additional evidence of the substantial overlap between social and physical pain. Current findings also suggest that people report higher levels of self-reported pain and have diminished performance on a cognitively demanding task after reliving a past socially meaningful but painful event more than a past physically painful event (Chen, Williams, Fitness, & Newton, 2008).

Finally, research on individual positive psychological well-being (Schwartz, Reyonolds, Thase, Frank, Fasiczka, & Haaga, 2002), success in marriage (Gottman, 1994) and team effectiveness (Losada & Heaphy, 2004) suggest that the ratio of positive-to-negative emotions and interactions is of critical importance. For example, Losada and Heaphy (2004) unobtrusively observed actual work teams working on strategic planning tasks and coded all interpersonal interactions as positive (e.g., demonstrations of support and encouragement) or negative (e.g., cynicism and disapproval of others).

They identified 15 flourishing teams defined as showing uniformly high performance across three indicators: profitability, customer satisfaction, and evaluations by superiors, peers, and subordinates. Other teams were categorized as mixed (n=26) or low performers (n=19). Losada and Heaphy (2004) found that the optimally performing teams demonstrated an approximate 3:1 positive-to-negative ratio of interpersonal interactions, but performance decreased at 11.9:1 (i.e., teams became more dysfunctional and less productive suggesting a possible upper limit of positive-to-negative interactions). Despite some recent criticisms of this study (Fredrickson, 2013), a ratio of 3:1 positive –to-negative interactions appears to be significantly associated with enhanced individual and team performance, individual engagement, emotional flourishing, and effectiveness (Fredrickson, 2013; Fredrickson & Losada, 2005).

Neurobiological research hints that perceptions around status, certainty, autonomy, social relationships, and fairness (Rock, 2008) can possibly derail a 360-degree feedback process and create emotional stress in employees which can potentially interfere with insight, acceptance, and initial motivation to change behavior. The positivity-to-negativity ratio studies mentioned earlier are important to consider in light of how employees experience and interpret ratings and comments from others in a 360-degree feedback process. In particular, a preponderance of negative (versus positive) feedback messages can interfere with both proximal (insight and motivation) and distal goals (sustained deliberate practice and overall effectiveness) in the coaching engagement.

5. Does 360-degree feedback work (for whom and under what conditions)?

Among researchers and consultants, there is little disagreement that under the right conditions and applying evidence-based "best practices" that 360-degree feedback can increase self-awareness and increase individual and team effectiveness (Nowack & Mashihi, 2012; Fleenor, Taylor, & Craig, 2008; Reilly, Smither, & Vasilopoulos, 1996). At this point, there appears to be a need for even more in-depth prospective studies that allow for a more complete evaluation of the impact of 360-feedback interventions along with potential limits of behavioral change. An earlier meta-analysis of 26 longitudinal studies by Smither, London, and Reilly (2005) suggests that 360-degree feedback does lead to significant improvements on both perceptions of improved performance and actual behavioral change and some insights about the conditions required to ensure success.

In their meta-analysis, Smither et al., (2005) examined the mean unweighted (and uncorrected) effect sizes and compared them to the mean weighted (and uncorrected) effect sizes. The mean unweighted (and uncorrected) effect sizes were .24, .12, .14, and .00 for direct report, peer, supervisor, and self-ratings, respectively. The mean weighted (and uncorrected) effect sizes were .12, .04, .10 and .03 for direct report, peer, supervisor, and self-ratings, respectively. Across rater sources (excluding self-ratings), the average effect size in the developmental purpose studies was .25 versus .08 in the administrative purpose studies.

It is important to note that 15 of the 24 studies included in the meta-analytic calculated only a single score (i.e., the average rating across all items). Smither et al., (2005) also noted whether the study involved only upward feedback (i.e., only from direct reports) versus feedback from multiples sources (i.e., direct reports, peers, supervisor) as well as being used for developmental purposes or for personnel decisions (e.g., promotion decisions, performance reviews). The authors point out that these small effect sizes might be influenced by averaging ratings across all items at Time 1 versus Time 2 (over half of the studies in their meta-analysis. They suggest a shift to evaluating change in goal progress or behavioral effectiveness might be more appropriate to measure the true impact of 360-degree interventions.

A recent meta-analysis of coaching engagement (Jones et al., 2015) explored diverse outcomes in 17 specific organizational studies. Results indicated that coaching had positive and significant effects on organizational outcomes overall ($d = 0.36$), and on specific forms of outcome criteria (skill-based $d= 0.28$; affective $d = 0.51$; individual-level results $d=1.24$). However, coaching was significantly more effective when 360-degree feedback was not included in the coaching engagement ($d = 0.88$ vs. $d = 0.21$). The non-overlapping confidence intervals found in this study suggests that coaching has a stronger overall impact when it is provided without multisource feedback. The authors offer several possible explanations for their results. First, they suggest that employees might be pre-occupied by the content of the feedback during the coaching sessions (e.g., negative feedback). Second, they suggest that the relevance of the actual 360-degree feedback might be distal to the actual goals of the coaching engagement.

Overall, these findings suggest that expected performance improvements may be practically modest for even those most motivated and capable of changing behavior over time (Smither, et al., 2005). Taken together, there is supporting evidence that feedback is a necessary and important condition for successful behavioral change and most useful for those employees with moderate to low levels of self-insight, or who express a strong motivation to improve, demonstrate poor performance on teachable skills, and have a learning versus performance goal orientation (Leonardelli, Herman, Lynch, & Arkin, 2003).

Smither et al., (2005) presented eight important factors that play a role in determining the extent of behavioral change and performance improvement following 360-degree feedback interventions. These factors help answer questions related to for whom and under what conditions feedback can be most beneficial and impactful. The eight factors include: (1) the delivery and content of the feedback; (2) interpretations and emotional reactions to feedback; (3) the personality of the participant; (4) feedback orientation of the participant; (5) readiness to change, (6) beliefs about change as well as self-esteem and self-efficacy; (7) goal intentions versus implementation intentions; and (8) taking/ sustaining action while managing possible relapse.

It would appear that these factors would be useful for consultants to consider and for researchers to continue to focus on improving the efficacy of feedback interventions for individuals, teams, and organizations. For example, consultants who can identify their employee's readiness for change level and evaluate important personality variables related to acceptance of the feedback, achievement orientation, and openness to change (e.g., conscientiousness, emotional stability) will be better able to tailor their approach to discussing the feedback results and setting development goals.

Additionally, consultants should help define, clarify, and focus employee development goals and translate them to implementation intentions to maximize successful behavioral change and help strategize possible coping strategies to minimize potential relapse (Mashihi & Nowack, 2011; Nowack, 2005). Finally, in light of the recent meta-analysis by Jones et al. (2015), it would appear that best practices be used when including 360-degree feedback in coaching engagements to both manage potential negative emotional reactions following feedback and to help translate insight into deliberate practice.

6. *Should 360-degree feedback ever be used for performance appraisal and compensation?*

In a recent 2009 survey of over 50 companies by the 3D group, 32 percent reported using 360 degree feedback for administrative as well as development purposes and 68 percent reported using it only for development. Only 16 percent reported that 360-degree feedback was directly linked to pay increases. 360-degree feedback can support performance appraisal systems but should cautiously be linked to remuneration and compensation systems (Fleenor, Taylor & Chappelow, 2008). For example, the generation of an individual performance development plan is typically a strategic part of most performance-appraisal systems. The use of 360-degree feedback assessment as part of developmental planning can strengthen existing performance-management and appraisal systems. When 360-degree feedback is used in compensation, it is difficult to know which rater group to use (e.g., manager ratings are significantly higher than direct reports) and how to evaluate within-rater agreement. The type of rating and response scale should also be appropriate for the intended purpose (e.g., not using a potential scale for compensation decisions).

7. *What do you do if the organizational culture isn't ready for 360-feedback interventions?*

Not all organizations are ready to use 360-degree feedback systems, or the time such a feedback system is introduced may not be optimum to ensure success. For example, it is not recommended to introduce a 360-degree feedback process in the middle of a very large organizational change. It is highly recommended that 360-degree feedback systems should be piloted by a willing stakeholder or a group that is open to giving and receiving feedback. Often, the use of a "180-degree feedback" process between an employee and his or her manager is a wonderful way to softly introduce the benefits of a full-blown, 360-degree feedback to the organization. In order to succeed, employees need to feel comfortable with the feedback process, and they need to believe they will be given honest, constructive, and useful feedback. Finally, 360-degree feedback processes should be used to solve real business needs. In this way, such feedback is introduced as a solution for improving leadership effectiveness or team building. Some key questions to ask to determine if your culture is ready for the successful introduction and use of 360-degree feedback interventions include:

- Is employee engagement high enough to support a feedback intervention?
- Is the organization supportive of talent development and coaching?
- Do managers get trained, rewarded, and compensated if they act as performance consultants?
- Do employees feel comfortable giving feedback without reprisal?
- Has your organization had a bad experience with a prior 360-degree feedback intervention?

- Is talent motivated to use the feedback it receives for its own professional growth and development?
- Does your organization have resources, training, and other support in place to help talent create and implement professional development plans as a result of the feedback?
- Will talent be held accountable to discuss the results of feedback with bosses and to create a development plan?

8. *Is 360-degree feedback ever inappropriate?*

Use caution in going forward with 360-degree feedback processes under the following situations: 1) if the person participating in 360-degree feedback is very new to the organization, 2) if there are not enough respondents who truly understand the full scope of the individual's responsibilities, 3) if you are in a time of major organizational change or a transition, such as just before or after a merger or acquisition, and 4) if you are in an organizational culture, climate, or environment where there is a high degree of mistrust.

9. *How do you ensure 360-degree feedback success?*

Current research on "best practices" in the use of 360 degree feedback (Nowack, 2009) suggests that results can be optimized if you understand the following principles: 1) Hold the participant and line manager accountable for creating, implementing and completing a development plan, 2) Provide individual coaching to assist in interpreting the multi-rater feedback, 3) Link the 360-degree feedback intervention to a performance-management process, 4) Target competencies for 360-degree feedback interventions related to strategic business needs; and 5) Build in mechanisms to evaluate progress of both the completion of development plans and effectiveness of newly practiced behaviors/ skills.

Figure 5-3

Assessment / Competencies

10. What competencies should be measured?
11. How independent are competencies?
12. How do you go about developing competencies for a 360-degree feedback assessment?
13. What type and how many raters should be included?
14. Do ratings between rater groups agree with each other?
15. Do ratings within rater groups agree with each other?
16. What is the optimum length of a 360-degree assessment?
17. What kind of response scale should you use?
18. How many rating points should be on a 360-degree scale?
19. How do you label response scales in 360-degree assessments?
20. Do the 360-degree feedback questions and competencies have adequate reliability and validity?
21. Is a customized 360-degree feedback assessment better than a vendor's off-the-shelf assessment?
22. How do I write good behavioral statements for 36-degree feedback assessments?
23. How many behavioral statements should I have for each competency?

ASSESSMENT AND COMPETENCIES

10. *How many and what competencies should be measured?*

The type and number of competencies measured for a 360-degree feedback assessment should be based on a theoretical model, a particular job level, or the core, strategic competencies required of an organization to be successful in its competitive market. It is also important to consider the ability of raters to make reliable and discriminate judgments about behaviors they are rating. In general, there is tremendous overlap between vendor job level competency models based on interviews, focus groups, and survey approaches in identifying job-related skills, abilities, and success factors.

In a meta-analytic review of the criterion-related validity of assessment centers by Arthur et al. (2003), the mean number of competencies measured by raters was 10.60. The authors emphasize that a much smaller number of competencies may adequately explain the variance in performance outcomes. It is important to note that in assessment centers, raters (assessors) are typically carefully selected, motivated and trained to evaluate observed performance without ever knowing the participant. In 360-degree feedback processes, raters might not be fully motivated or skilled at making behavioral ratings suggesting that minimizing the overall number of competencies to be evaluated might actually enhance reliability and accuracy of ratings although little research exists to determine the optimum number of competencies to be measured. The exact number of competencies being measured might be less of an issue if they are job relevant and the items being measured are behaviorally based and clear to the rater.

For example, the competency model behind the Envisia Learning, Inc. *Executive View 360* was based on job analysis interviews with senior level executives from several diverse industries, resulting in a total of 22 competencies grouped into four areas associated with executive success: 1) performance leadership, 2) change leadership, 3) interpersonal leadership, and 4) intrapersonal leadership. This executive to be useful for executive coaching, talent/succession planning and training programs focused on enhancing one or more competencies.

11. *How independent are competencies?*

Research studies on 360-degree feedback have consistently shown high intercorrelations *among* competencies, and as such, there may be some justification for research purposes to combine all competencies into an overall outcome measure (e.g., leadership). However, for developmental or coaching purposes, it is desirable to maintain the competency architecture and the model behind the assessment to support the feedback and developmental planning process, in light of findings that the overlap in competencies, although significant, only accounts for about 50 percent of the variance. At a practical level for coaching and developmental purpose, treating each competency separately can be supported.

12. *How do you go about developing competencies for a 360-degree feedback assessment?*

Competencies are those KSAOs (knowledge, skills, abilities, and other attributes) that differentiate between high and low performers (McClelland, 1961). However, the term competencies is often confused with other terms, including dimensions, KSAOs, success factors or profiles, leadership traits, and core competencies. Several approaches to competency-model development include:

- Analyzing company information
- Utilizing existing competency models
- Conducting incumbent or subject matter expert (SMEs) interviews and focus groups
- Conducting job and family KSAO surveys

Competency modeling steps typically include the following:

1. *Performance criteria:* defining the criteria for superior performance in a role, position, or job level.

2. *Criterion sample:* choosing a sample of people performing the role for data collection and/or SMEs.

3. *Data collection:* collecting sample data about behaviors that lead to success.

4. *Data analysis:* developing hypotheses about the competencies of outstanding performers and how these competencies work together to produce desired results.

5. *Validation:* validating the results of data collection and analysis.

6. *Application:* applying the competency models in human resource systems.

13. *What type and how many raters should be included?*

The type of raters who provide feedback to clients will depend on a number of factors, including the purpose of the 360-degree feedback process, the job level of the client, the competencies being assessed, and the relevant stakeholders who had an opportunity to provide constructive feedback. In general, 360-degree feedback processes typically include the client's manager, direct reports, team members (different job levels), peers (same job level), or others. Each rater type appears to provide unique and meaningful information and may become a focal point for developmental actions (Fleenor et al., 2008).

How many raters are necessary to provide meaningful and accurate 360-degree feedback? The answer, of course, is only one rater, but there is no way to know who is "all-knowing" and perfectly accurate in his or her observations. The following analogy demonstrates this. Sit down with a child to solve a puzzle and ask this question; "How many puzzle pieces do you need to assemble to have confidence that what you are making resembles the picture on the cover?" The more puzzle pieces we assemble correctly, the more confident we become that we are seeing the image that is also on the cover of the box. There is no need to assemble all of the pieces to verify this. All that is needed is a "critical mass" of puzzle pieces of the assembled puzzle pieces to be confident of the true picture of the puzzle.

When clients ask raters for feedback, it is hoped that they have a clear and accurate picture of how they are behaving and being perceived by others. In fact, there is some research that suggests what this "critical mass" of feedback is in order to reach a level of confidence that others are accurately experiencing the client's behavior and can identify signature strengths and development opportunities. Greguras and Robie (1995) suggested that the optimum number of raters requires at least four supervisors, eight peers, and nine direct reports to achieve acceptable levels of reliability (.70 or higher). Of course, this statistical standard may not be practical in circumstances in which leaders have only a few direct reports or when the input of only the current manager is desired.

Recent research suggests that when two or fewer respondents provide data for a given group, this small number of rater responses may be inadequate for reliable measurement (3D Group, 2009). Inviting more, rather than fewer, raters would be helpful in ensuring accuracy and a large enough rater pool to make the 360-degree feedback findings relevant and useful. Inviting and having too few raters in each rater category may limit the meaningfulness and accuracy of the feedback for professional and personal development.

One study (Nieman-Gonder, Metlay, Kaplan, & Wolfe, 2006) has explored ratings provided by selected and non-selected raters by clients using multiple accuracy measures. Results indicated that selected raters were as accurate, or more accurate, than raters who were not selected by the client. Therefore, having a critical mass of feedback is essential whether raters are nominated by the client and without input from others or selected directly by human resources or the client's manager.

Ideally, the selection of both the number and type of raters should be a participative process between the client and his or her manager to optimize acceptance of the feedback results (Bracken & Rose, 2011).

14. *Do ratings* between *rater groups agree with each other?*

There is an extensive literature on the relationship between rater reliability and job performance that has implications for expecting and interpreting differences between rater groups in 360-degree feedback (Le, Oh, Shaffer, & Schmidt, 2007; Murphy, 2008; Murphy, Cleveland, & Mohler, 2001). Whereas high levels of interrater reliability are necessary for adequate measurement in most performance evaluation systems, 360-degree feedback interventions are based on the assumption that raters from different levels provide unique and meaningful information (Lance et al., 2008). From this perspective, some degree of cross-source disagreement is actually desirable, and source effects are not necessarily an indicator of poor quality ratings (Hoffman & Woehr, 2009). For example, Wanguri (1995) found that multiple rater appraisals improved rating accuracy and perceptions of fairness in a meta-analysis of 113 empirical studies on performance evaluations.

Some research suggests that findings of low levels of agreement across rating sources may be largely spurious. Specifically, Libretto, Burgess, Kaiser, Archly, and James (2003) present a convincing case that estimates of inter-rater agreement based on intraclass and Pearson correlations are severely attenuated because of restriction of range in job performance and thus represent substantial underestimates of interpreter agreement. Scullen, Mount, and Goff (2000), hypothesized that observed variations in ratings might reflect actual differences in performance because an employee is likely to perform differentially in front of diverse groups of people.

They suggest that rating differences are more a function of true differences in the observed performance than of variations in the observers themselves (bias). Their study found small perspective-related effects were observed in boss andsubordinate ratings, but not in peer ratings.

Other researchers also support the use of multiple independent raters who have had opportunity to observe ratee performance and pooling of performance ratings across raters to improve reliability of rating scores on which organizational decisions may be based (Murphy, 2008; Ones, Viswesvaran, & Schmidt, 2008; Viswesvaran, Schmidt, & Ones, 2002; 2005). These findings suggest that different rater sources, including self-ratings, represent valid performance-related variance and most likely are not mere measurement method bias (Hoffman, Lance, Bynum, & Gentry, 2010). It is also important to note that inter-rater agreement and inter-rater reliability can, but do not necessarily coexist (Liao, Hunt, & Chen, 2010). The presence of one does not ensure the other. Inter-rater agreement and inter-rater reliability are both important for the accuracy and usefulness of performance evaluation. The former indicates stability of ratings an employee receives from different raters, while the latter shows the consistency of ratings across different employees from different raters.

In general, self-ratings have been found to be modestly correlated to other rater perspectives (Pearson correlations .3 to .6), with a greater convergence between peer and supervisor ratings (Conway & Huffcutt 1997; Harris & Schaubreck, 1988; Nowack, 1992; 2002). Cumulative evidence suggests that supervisors are the most reliable source of job performance ratings (Conway & Huffcutt, 1997) and their ratings are more strongly associated with performance as measured by external criteria (e.g., promotions, salary) than are ratings from other sources (Atkins & Wood, 2002; Beehr, Ivanitskaya, Hansen, Erofeev & Gudanowski, 2001). Findings from Viswesvaran, Schmidt, and Ones (2005) also suggest that supervisory ratings of overall job performance are empirically related to other measurements of job performance.

In general, supervisors tend to focus more on performance-oriented behaviors compared to direct reports who tend to emphasize and filter interpersonal and relationship behaviors into subjective ratings (Nowack, 2009). Despite some mixed evidence (e.g., Sala & Dwight, 2002), peers are able to discern future leadership potential (Nowack, 2009), leadership efficacy (Chemers, Watson, & May, 2000; Hannah, Avolio, Luthans, & Harms, 2008), accurately evaluate job performance (Law, Wong, & Song, 2004), and are particularly sensitive to negatively evaluate the personality trait of narcissism in others (Goffin & Anderson, 2007).

For example, Inceoglu and Externbrink (2012) collected data for 151 international managers from a global Fortune 500 company (consumer goods sector) who participated in an internal leadership program. Results showed that assessment center (AC) ratings correlated positively with 360-degree feedback ratings for the same competency but only if rated by peers. Overlap between 360-degree feedback and overall AC ratings made by independent assessors in this managerial sample shows that peers may have a more accurate perspective of a participant's performance compared to subordinates or managers. In their analysis of leadership effectiveness with 74 executives using 360-degree feedback, Harris & Kuhnert (2007) reported that peers' evaluations added incremental information distinct from superiors in predicting overall leadership effectiveness.

These meaningful rater group differences might also be a point of possible confusion in the interpretation of 360-degree assessments for employees trying to use these results to determine specific behaviors to modify for some or all rater groups (e.g., their boss and/or direct reports). This potential ambiguity in understanding and interpreting 360-degree feedback is important in light of recent research suggesting that people who are even mildly neurotic report more distress by uncertainty within oral and written feedback than when given very direct negative feedback (Hirsh & Inzlicht, 2008).

At a practical level, employees might be challenged to understand how to interpret important differences observed by rater groups and to decide whether to focus development efforts on managing upward, downward, or laterally in light of potentially discrepant results. Consultants should be cognizant of the moderate correlations between different rater groups and help their employees to fully understand and interpret the meaning of such differences.

For example, if an employee receives a report showing low ratings from both the employee's manager and peers but much higher ratings from direct reports, the coach might explore the current relationship with the employee's boss as well as the meaningfulness of the discrepancies in ratings by those they directly supervise and work with at a peer level. Because peers seem to focus on "followership" traits such as self-esteem, ability to accept feedback, and confidence in their ratings (Goffin & Anderson, 2007), these co-worker relationships might need to be nurtured and strengthened for employees who have aspirations for seeking future leadership opportunities within the organization. HR practitioners should also be familiar with the findings of Brett and Atwater (2001) who reported that participants in their 360-degree feedback program had stronger emotional reactions to negative feedback from bosses and peers than they did to negative feedback from direct reports.

It appears that almost all vendors who generate 360-degree feedback reports present various ways to compare and contrast self-versus other rater responses (e.g., graphs or tables showing average scores across competencies and specific behaviors). However, it is typically up to the employee to discern the meaning of these differences and what actions, if any, should be considered as a result of the feedback they received. Correctly interpreting and acting on these perceptual differences by rater groups is both an opportunity and challenge inherent in 360-degree feedback interventions.

15. *Do ratings* within *rater groups agree with each other?*

In an earlier meta-analytic study of 360-degree feedback performance ratings by Conway and Huffcutt (1997), the average correlation between two supervisors was only .50, for peers, it was .37, and between two subordinates, it was only .30. Until a newer meta-analytic review is conducted, it would appear that agreement within rater groups appears to be an important issue to discern for employees in the interpretation of their 360-degree feedback reports.

Several explanations have been offered as to why different raters of the same individual may provide discrepant ratings including:

1) raters selectively focus on different aspects of an individual's competence, personality, and/or performance; 2) raters have different opportunities to actually observe and experience the behavior of others (e.g., sampling bias); 3) raters attribute different levels of importance to the same observed behavior influencing the way they make appraisals of others; and 4) the linguistic characteristics of the actual questions in 360-degree assessments influence rater appraisals (Lebreton, Burgess, Kaiser, Atchley, & James, 2003; Kaiser & Craig, 2005).

For example, using an archival database of responses (N=737), a study by Dai, Stiles, Hallenbeck, and De Meuse (2007) found that when a leadership competency was abstract, the agreement between self and others was lower than if the competency was concrete. Kaiser et al., (2005) argued that vendors and companies developing 360-degree feedback assessments should pay special attention to the specific questions being asked (e.g., behaviorally specific, placed in a proper context and not double barreled) to enhance interrater reliability.

Vendors who do not provide a way for employees to evaluate within-rater group agreement in feedback may increase the probability that average scores used in reports can be easily be misinterpreted— particularly if they are used by consultants to help employees focus on specific competencies and behaviors for developmental planning purposes. It is not unusual for employees to expend a great deal of energy trying to identify their potential "critics" and "supporters" in discussing the results of the 360-degree feedback assessment when there is discrepancy of ratings within rater categories (e.g., direct reports).

Having a way to discern and discuss potential "outliers" in the data can help employees be more focused on their developmental goals and make informed choices about how much energy to put into "managing" their direct reports, peers, or boss.

From a practical perspective, vendors should provide one or more measures of rater agreement within each individual feedback report such as: 1) Including a range of scores on self-other rating summaries; 2) Showing a distribution of ratings on most and least frequent behavior summaries in a manner that ensures confidentiality; and 3) Including statistical metrics of rater agreement (e.g., based on standard deviation or standard error). All of these within-rater group agreement metrics would appear to help delineate potential outliers and clarify how to possibly interpret polarized scores at both a competency and question level.

It is easy for employees to review a 360-degree feedback report including a table ranking the most or least frequently observed behaviors (e.g., based on the calculation of average scores by rater groups) and immediately interpret specific behaviors on which to focus their development efforts. Employees often do so without an analysis of whether the average scores might truly reflect rater "clans" of supporters and critics that require additional follow-up to clarify what the average scores may mean. Having at least one approach in 360-degree feedback reports to measure and evaluate within-rater agreement, without breaking confidentiality, would appear useful for accurately interpreting results and facilitating meaningful development planning. When there are only a few raters who provide feedback to an employee, the possibility of an "outlier" magnifies the importance of interpreting average scores at the item level cautiously

16. *What is the optimum length of a 360-degree feedback assessment?*

In general, 360-degree feedback questionnaires should be targeted and contain relevant questions. They should be long enough to accurately measure the competencies they are attempting to assess, but not too long as to decrease the motivation to complete them. It takes, on average, between 30 and 60 seconds to answer each question, and if a respondent is asked to complete questionnaires on a number of people, it is important that respondent fatigue doesn't set in. Typically, 360-degree feedback questionnaires contain between 40 and 70 items along with several open-ended questions. They often can be completed in 10-15 minutes. In a recent 2009 survey of over 50 companies by the 3D group (3D Group, 2009 Benchmark Study) the "sweet spot" for the number of questions in a 360-degree feedback questionnaire appeared to between 11 to 40 (33 percent) and 41 to 69 (42 percent). A total of 16 percent of the 50 companies surveyed had questionnaires that had 70 or more questions.

17. *Which response scale is best for 360-degree feedback?*

Many studies suggest that response scales have an impact on the 360-degree feedback data and some response scales seem to be preferable to others (Heidemeier & Moser, 2009; Viswesvaran, Bergen, Dutta, & Childres, 1996). For example, Bracken and Rose (2011) suggest that commonly used frequency scales (e.g., never to always) are inferior to others (e.g., satisfaction or effectiveness) because of lack of variability in the responses, but are quick to point out that the majority of research has focused on the anchors themselves and additional research is needed to identify optimal response choices and/or anchor format.

A recent meta-analysis by Heidemeier and Moser (2009) suggested that social comparison scales (scales with relative rather than absolute anchors) were able to reduce leniency in self-ratings and should be employed much more often than in the past. Goffin and Olson (2011) also presented evidence from at least three important and quite different domains that comparative evaluative judgments of the self or others (i.e., whether a given person is higher or lower on some characteristic than is another specific person) may be more advantageous than absolute evaluative judgments (i.e., asking the respondent to indicate the individual's level of performance, attitude, traits, or other attributes using numerical scales with verbal anchors such as low to high, unfavorable to favorable, bad to good).

Hoffman, Gorman, Blair, Meriac, Overstreet, & Atchley (2012) explored a new method of presenting items in 360-degree feedback assessments called frame-of-reference scales (FORS) in both a laboratory and field-based study. Drawing from previous approaches to improve the quality of performance ratings, Frame of Reference Scales (FORS) add definitions and examples of effective and ineffective behaviors to a set of behavioral items associated with each dimension or competency being assessed (i.e., provides behavioral examples on the scale itself with a few critical anchors). They found that FORS were associated with a higher pattern of competency factor loadings, less overlap, and decrease of error in measurement (Hoffman et al., 2012). The overall impact of using this FORS scaling approach in both studies was found to be moderate in overall effect size but a significant improvement over the use of traditional rating scales and, as such, deserves additional research attention.

Holt and Seki (2012) encouraged vendors and consultants to explore alternative assessment approaches and scaling that will be more culturally sensitive to defining, measuring, and evaluating leadership competence in light of the use of 360-degree feedback within multi-national companies. They encouraged consideration of alternatives beyond frequency-based scales that might emphasize perceptions of overdoing or underdoing behaviors (e.g., Kaiser & Overfield, 2011) and bi-polar scales measuring strengths and the overuse of those strengths.

Gentry and Eckert (2012) suggested that using a dual scale of leadership expectations (ratings on the dimensions that contribute or hinder leadership in general) and perceptions (actual ratings of behavior) and exploring the alignment between these two might also improve and enhance cross-cultural measurement and development of employees receiving feedback. They argued that this method differs from traditional 360-degree measurement approaches in that perceptions per se, are neutral and that meaning is dependent on the context of "local" expectations. Therefore, the "fit" between expectations and perceptions helps consultants interpret the results with their employee. They also pointed out some limitations of this approach such as overload of data to interpret for the employee and how expectations of raters may shift over time (e.g., changing roles or styles of leaders required to remain competitive in the marketplace).

A recent review of the literature suggests that there are diverse approaches to the use of response scales in 360-degree feedback assessments (e.g., comparison versus absolute). In general, response or rating scales are important to consider when developing customized 360-degree feedback assessments and interpreting off-the-shelf tools available from vendors.

People usually define their strengths based on traits they already possess and define their developmental opportunities more in terms of abilities they lack (Dunning, Heath, & Suls, 2004). Kaiser & Overfield (2011) found that leaders were five times more likely to overdo behaviors related to their strengths and that most 360-degree feedback assessments do not "distinguish doing a lot of a behavior from doing too much of it or distinguish underdoing from overdoing as two distinct classes of performance problems" (pp. 105-106).

The selection and use of 360-degree feedback scales should be properly matched to the purposes of their use (e.g., development emphasizing what employees can translate into deliberate practice, selection/succession planning which typically depends on comparing employees ratings to others or performance evaluation which may require a mix of the two Researchers should continue to explore and investigate the use of alternative 360-degree scales to maximize cross-culture relevance and meaningful interpretation of results. Practitioners using 360-degree feedback assessments should also consider providing employee and rater training which is generally accepted as an effective method to enhance the psychometric soundness of ratings (Hoffman & Baldwin, 2012; Woehr, 2008).

Various types of evaluative social judgments about the self or others (e.g., employee job performance ratings, self-reported attitudes, ratings of others' in 360-degree feedback) may be obtained more accurately using comparative ratings rather than absolute ratings. Comparative ratings involve relative judgments of a person in comparison with other individuals or groups, whereas absolute ratings involve judgments of a person on scales that do not explicitly reference other people (Wagner & Goffin, 1997; Goffin & Olson, 2011).

Regarding serial (one ratee evaluated by a rater at time) or parallel (one behavior evaluated across all participants by the rater at one time), Jelley et al., (2012) concluded that a serial approach was generally more accurate than a parallel approach. Despite perceptions from employees that using a parallel approach appear faster and easier to do, a serial approach to completing 360-degree feedback assessments seems well suited for developmental purposes (Jelley et al., 2012).

18. *How many rating points should be on a 360-degree feedback scale?*

There is no definitive agreement from researchers or vendors about the optimal number of response categories that should be used in order to get the most reliable data in 360-degree assessments. However, there is a general range provided in the broader survey literature that suggests the number of response categories to consider using (Cicchetti, Showalter, & Tyrer, 1985; Cools, Hofmans, &Theuns, 2006; Dawes, 2008; Wikman & Warneryd, 1990; Weng, 2004). The most recent findings from a 2009 benchmark study (3D Group, 2009) suggest that the most popular in practice is a 5-point scale (76 percent) followed by a 7-point rating scale (16 percent).

For example, Bandalos and Enders (1996) found that the reliability was highest for scales having five to seven points. Preston and Colman (2000) examined response categories ranging from two to eleven, and reported that test-retest reliability was lowest for two to four point scales and was highest for seven to 10 point scales (there was a noted decrease beyond 10 response categories). In a direct comparison of the reliability and validity of 4-point and 6-point Likert scales, Chang (2005) found that criterion-related validity was not affected by the number of scale points but reliability was higher using the 4-point scale.

Research by Lozano, Garcia-Cueto, and Muniz (2008) also investigated the reliability and validity of scales ranging from two to nine response options with four different sample sizes. Their analyses suggested that having between four and seven response options was optimal. It is important to note that the number of rating points may be largely dependent on the type of scale being used (e.g., frequency, effectiveness, comparison) and/or a selection of using a curvilinear approach such as the "too little versus too much" frequency scale discussed by Kaiser and Overfield (2011).

New research confirms that the "sweet spot" for 360-degree feedback response scales is between four and seven for both commercial and organizationally developed assessments (3D Group, 2009). Current research suggests that short (less than three) and long (greater than seven) response scales are generally less reliable and popular in practice.

Consultants should make sure that the response scale is appropriate for the purpose of the 360-degree feedback intervention (e.g., development versus personnel decisions) and understand the implications for interpretation of results when the full range of the response scale is not used by most raters (e.g., negative skewness). For example, some evidence suggests that standard deviations are larger across all competencies with the use of positively worded response scales (i.e., those that include more positive than negative labels as rating descriptors) in 360-degree feedback assessments (English, Rose, & McClellan, 2009). The use of positively worded response scales might be useful to increase variability in rater responses increasing accuracy and making interpretation of feedback results more meaningful for employees.

19. *How do you best label 360-degree feedback rating scales?*

An important issue for response scales is considering how to best label the response scale anchors. Weng (2004) analyzed the *reliability* of Likert-type rating scales and found that scales with all response options clearly labeled yielded higher test-retest reliability than those with only the end-points labeled. This suggests that having all of the points on a scale clearly labeled help reduce ambiguity. Cools, Hofmans, and Theuns (2006) found that a scale with five response options was the least prone to context effects and that the use of extreme answer categories on the left and right ends of the scale *did not* improve the psychometric properties of the scale. Viswanathan, Bergen, Dutta, and Childres (1996) in studying the optimal number of response categories and appropriate category descriptors found that the right number of categories was important, so that there was not a mismatch between participants' natural responses and the response categories.

Leniency effects (negative skew or low variability) in scale ratings are fairly common in 360-degree feedback. Few raters use the entire rating scale range, and most scores tend to be inflated, independent of the scale being used. Recent research suggests that the use of *positively worded* scales can result in *lower mean scores and increased variability,* relative to typical, anchored scales (English, Rose, & McClellan, 2009) Positive-worded scales are comprised of anchors with a larger number of positive verbal qualifiers and should be considered for coaches, consultants, and organizations creating their own customized 360-degree feedback assessments.

Example of a Traditional Frequency Scale

    1: To a very small extent
    2: To a small extent
    3: To a moderate extent
    4: To a large extent
    5: To a very large extent

Example of a Positively-Worded Response Scale

    1: Almost never
    2: Sometimes
    3: Frequently
    4: Almost always
    5: Always

20. *Do the 360-degree feedback questions and competencies have adequate reliability and validity?*

There are many different types of reliability and validity. Ideally, a customized 360-degree feedback questionnaire should have established scale reliability (e.g., Cronbach's alpha greater than .70) to ensure that the questions are accurately measuring a single concept. It would also be useful to know whether the customized questionnaire had acceptable test-retest reliability.

Validity is also important for 360-degree feedback questionnaires. There are many different types of validity, so it is easy to be confused when someone says that his or her 360-degree feedback tool is valid. Minimally, a customized questionnaire should have "face validity," so that participants and raters tend to believe the questions and competencies are relevant to the purpose and goals of the feedback process.

It is possible to establish face validity by running a focus group with a representative group from within your organization or by piloting the 360-degree feedback questionnaire before a wider roll-out. It is important to establish whether the 360-degree feedback questions are clear and can be answered, whether the questionnaire itself is relevant to the individuals participating in the 360-degree feedback project, and whether all of the organization's key competencies are being measured.

Other kinds of validity that should be considered in the development of a customized 360-degree feedback assessment include criterion-related validity (does the customized instrument actually predict anything meaningful like performance?) and convergent or divergent validity (does the customized instrument correlate with like and dislike measures?). Whether you create and develop your own or purchase a vendor's assessment, you should make sure of the following basic psychometric properties:

1. Test-retest reliability (scores remain stable over a very short period of time when administered again)

2. Internal consistency reliability (the competencies or scales have items that are highly interrelated with each other)

3. Face validity (the competency model and questions appear to make sense for the job level or purpose of the assessment at a face level)

4. Criterion-related validity (scores on the assessment are correlated at a significant level with a relevant outcome like job performance or satisfaction)

5. Convergent and divergent validity (the assessment scale or competency is associated with scales that are similar and not associated with scales that are different).

21. *Is a customized 360-feedback assessment better than a vendor's off-the-shelf assessment?*

Not necessarily. Well-designed and psychometrically-sound off-the-shelf 360-degree feedback questionnaires (such as those available from Envisia Learning, Inc.) can be used effectively if the behaviors are all relevant. If behaviors are not relevant to the organization, then completing the 360-degree feedback questionnaire could be difficult and will not give you the results you are looking for. A customized 360-degree feedback assessment can be useful if designed to fit your exact needs or to support unique organizational competency frameworks or strategic development objectives and initiatives.

22. *How do I write good behavioral statements to be used in 360-degree feedback assessments?*

Writing good behavioral statements for a customized 360-degree feedback assessment is critical to ensure that what is being measured is accurate and useful for developmental purposes. Here are some recommended tips to ensure your questions are specific, behavioral, and useful:

- Ask only one thing in each question
- Ask something that can be observed by others
- Write in a clear language and avoid terms that may not be obvious, such as jargon or technical terms
- Double check that the item is relevant to the competency area and verifies that the wording of the question matches the scale
- Utilize Envisia Learning, Inc.'s, *Custom View 360 Library* online system to select from an extensive item pool of over 2,000 questions

23. How many behavioral statements should I have in each competency?

To ensure reliability of a scale, a general rule of thumb is to have a *minimum of three* behaviors in a 360-degree assessment. In general, the more questions you have for each scale, the more internal consistency and reliability increases. However, it is important to make sure you have written questions to measure the full scope of the competency you are trying to measure, without increasing the length to such an extent that compliance to complete the assessment is diminished or your questions are redundant.

Figure 5-4

Process / Implementation

24. Who should receive feedback from assessments?
25. Who should select raters? Does it matter?
26. What kind of communication should be shared with participants, managers, and raters?
27. How should feedback be given?
28. How do you ensure confidentiality of raters?
29. Should human resources have the ability to identify raters selected and track assessment progress?
30. Should participant be told who completed questionnaires?
31. Are there differences between written and online assessments?
32. How do you roll out a 360-degree feedback initiative across an entire company or for a specific job level?
33. Can open-ended questions be emotionally damaging to participants?
34. Should you edit or delete critical or non-helpful open-ended questions?
35. Does a 360-degree feedback report require debriefing?
36. Should an individual 360-degree feedback report contain a mix of graphs, charts, tables, and responses to open-ended questions to?
37. What should you do if raters don't agree with their results?
38. How should the 360-degree feedback data be collected?
39. Should participants share their 360-degree feedback results with others?
40. Do you need an external coach or facilitator to debrief and interpret 360-degree feedback reports?
41. Can 360-degree feedback be used together with personality and style
42. What is the typical 360-degree feedback project time schedule?
43. Should new employees be included in the feedback process?
44. Should participants inform respondents that they have been invited to give feedback?
45. How can employee development be facilitated?

PROCESS AND IMPLEMENTATION

24. *Who should receive feedback from the 360-degree assessments?*

The goal of all 360-degree feedback processes is to provide clear information for professional development in a manner that motivates individuals to make specific behavioral changes, leading to enhanced effectiveness. The feedback from 360-degree assessments can be shared with the program participant, his or her manager, and others within or outside the organization. The 360-degree feedback research suggests that the motivation for behavioral change is increased when feedback is perceived to be confidential and used for developmental purposes (Nowack, 2005).

Participants and raters who believe that feedback will be shared with others or believe that the process is not anonymous tend to inflate ratings or "game the system," making the information less objective and candid. However, what is most critical is to communicate and clarify the limits of confidentiality and anonymity and who will be receiving the actual results from any 360-degree feedback before the project is initiated.

25. *Who should select raters as part of a 360-degree feedback process?*

Selection of raters is important to ensure "buy in" and acceptance of the feedback results by participants because current research suggests that rater source factors explain (much) more variance in 360-degree feedback ratings whereas general performance explains (much) less variance than was previously believed (Hoffman, Lance, Bynum, & Gentry (2010). Typically, raters can be selected by program participants or they can be selected by management, or it can be a collaborative process between the participant and management.

In a recent study reviewing 360-degree feedback use in over 50 North American companies by the 3D Group (2009 Benchmark Study), 61 percent had participants select their own raters with manager approval, 31 percent allowed participants to select their own independently, 4 percent had human resources select raters, 2 percent had managers select raters and 2 percent reported some other process. When used for developmental purposes, research suggests that allowing participants to select their own raters may enhance feedback acceptance *without* reducing rater accuracy (Nieman-Gonder, 2006). Of course, for some purposes, such as performance appraisal or succession planning, having human resources select raters might be prudent and even recommended.

26. *What kind of communication should be shared with participants, managers, and raters?*

It is important to communicate clearly to all stakeholders involved in a 360-degree feedback process. Communication can take place face-to-face or via email and should cover such things as the purpose of the 360-degree feedback intervention, the deadline dates to collect data, confidentiality, who will receive the feedback report, and whom to contact for technical and administrative questions. It is desirable to meet with all participants, if possible, to discuss questions that they might have about the assessment and what raters they might want to invite for feedback.

Managers of the participants should be contacted about their role and responsibilities and about whether they will receive a copy of the feedback report or not. Raters should be informed about what type of feedback is being sought by participants, with assurances about anonymity and the volunteer nature of their participation.

If possible, it would be desirable to model the type of open-ended comments that are desirable (behaviorally-based, specific, non-evaluative) for the raters and to encourage raters to use the "Not Applicable" or "Not Observable" rating if they truly do not have enough information to accurately provide feedback to the participant.

27. How should the 360-degree feedback be given?

It is important that participants in a 360-degree feedback process be given a chance to interpret the final report in a manner that enhances the motivation to change behavior. Typically, feedback reports are returned to individuals during workshops or individual meetings, rather than simply mailed or e-mailed without facilitated discussion. In a large, corporate 360-degree evaluation study conducted by Envisia Learning, Inc., observed behavior change was greatest when feedback reports were facilitated by either an internal or external consultant (Nowack, 2005).

Research suggests that feedback should be facilitated by either internal or external facilitators or the participant's manager to ensure that the report is clearly understood and any potential negative reactions are managed. The use of internal or external facilitators can help focus on specific developmental areas and highlight specific training and developmental activities that might be most useful for the participant, based on the results and findings of the 360-degree feedback process.

28. How do you ensure the confidentiality and anonymity of raters?

Confidentiality is an important aspect of 360-degree feedback for both participants and respondents. It is necessary to ensure that everyone participates and feels able to answer honestly and candidly. If there are any doubts around confidentiality, then people will feel anxious about completing the questionnaire, and they'll be unsure of the purpose of the 360-degree feedback process or the use of the data. If respondents are not guaranteed that their 360-degree feedback responses are anonymous, then they may not provide accurate responses. In fact, research suggests that ratings are inflated when raters do not perceive their input is anonymous.

One approach that Envisia Learning, Inc., uses to ensure anonymity and confidentiality is called Anonymity *Protection (AP)*. On each project, the coach, consultant, or organization using our assessments can set the minimum number of raters in each specific rater group required in order for data from invited raters to be included in the summary feedback report. It is fairly common that data from a participant's manager will be shared openly, and the results from other rater groups are combined to ensure confidentiality. The *Anonymity Protection* level is often set on specific 360-degree feedback projects for direct reports, peers, and others at two to three, but this level depends on the size of the staff and team and the preferences of the coach or organization using the 360-degree feedback assessment.

29. *Should human resources or executives have the ability to identify the raters selected and track their progress?*

Human resources or executives might find it valuable to identify and select raters for particular goals in using 360-degree feedback, often for purposes of performance evaluation or talent management and succession planning. In most cases, 360-degree feedback sponsors should have the ability to track and monitor which raters participants have invited if they are empowered to select their own and to determine how many raters have completed the 360-degree assessments to ensure that the feedback results will include as many raters as possible. Envisia Learning provides an administrative tracking website for coaches, consultants, and human resources to monitor and track all 360-degree feedback projects and to help maximize the success of each feedback intervention.

30. *Should participants be told who has completed questionnaires?*

Much research verifies that when raters are held accountable or identified, they tend to inflate ratings on 360-degree feedback assessments, because they are concerned about the repercussions of low ratings. Thus, the anonymity of raters does appear to ensure more accurate ratings (Morgeson, Mumford, & Campion, 2005). Participants typically do know the responses of their own manager, but this is expected even in developmentally-oriented 360-degree feedback processes, because bosses typically provide evaluation of direct reports during performance reviews. At Envisia Learning, Inc., we share *how many* raters have completed the assessments but not *who* has completed the assessments to ensure the anonymity of raters providing feedback to each participant in a project. With this information, participants can send out reminders to all invited raters to increase participation or contact our organization for us to send out reminder e-mails to all raters who have not yet completed the assessment by a specific due date assigned on the project.

31. *Are there differences between handwritten and online assessments?*

The two most popular approaches for data collection are online or paper-and-pencil surveys. However, the majority of vendors and companies today utilize Internet-based administration systems, and several studies have verified that there is *equivalence* in using online methods, despite the ease of faking and response distortion that might be more easily controlled with the older paper-and-pencil approach (Penny 2003; Smither, Walker & Yap, 2004). However, the issues often raised of faking and response distortion, although still relevant, are less important, given that the majority of 360-degree feedback interventions are used for developmental purposes. It is important to keep in mind though that 360-feedback assessment used for developmental purposes and should not be constructed and administered as if they were a personnel test (e.g. making the questions transparent, linking questions to the competencies they measure, etc.).

32. *How do you best roll out a 360-degree feedback initiative across an entire company or job level?*

Ideally, it would be best to start at the most senior level that is sponsoring the leadership or talent development intervention to model the process and help facilitate leaders becoming better performance consultants. Without senior leadership support, most 360-degree feedback initiatives are doomed to fail, because participants are not held accountable for translating this feedback into development plans that can be reinforced by leaders in the organization (Nowack, 2009).

In large organizations, it is also important to consider the burden of completing large numbers of 360-degree feedback assessments at one time that might create rater fatigue, lack of candor, or diminished motivation to provide specific feedback. In these cases, organizations should consider "cascading" their 360-degree feedback project, so that small groups within departments or the organization begin the process at different times.

33. *Can open-ended questions be emotionally damaging to employees?*

It is common in most online based 360-degree feedback assessments to include one or more open-ended questions which are typically voluntarily and confidentially answered by raters (typically these comments are categorized by rater groups used in the assessment process or listed in a random order without reference to rater groups). In general, there has been little research evaluating the cognitive and emotional reactions of such qualitative feedback on employees in the 360-degree literature based on online data collection. Narrative comments shared by raters can possibly be evaluative, overly critical, or negative, having an adverse impact on acceptability and motivation if included in reports without editing or removal.

A study by Smither and Walker (2004) analyzed the impact of upward feedback ratings, as well as narrative comments, over a one-year period for 176 managers. The number of raters providing comments per target manager ranged from 1 to 12 (M = 3.10, SD = 2.21). The number of comments per target manager ranged from 1 to 35 (M = 7.35, SD = 6.14). Seventy percent of the comments were coded as 3.5 or higher (1 = unfavorable, 5 = favorable). The study found that those who received a small number of unfavorable, behaviorally-based comments improved significantly more than other managers, but those who received a large number (relative to positive comments) significantly declined in performance more than other managers (Smither et al.,

2004). Unfortunately, the study did not quantify the exact number or ratio of negative to positive comments that might be the "tipping point" for performance declines.

When the 3:1 ratio of positive-to-negative open-ended comments begins to decrease and be of a magnitude that could create strong emotional reactions on the part of employees (Losada, et al., 2009), consultants face a set of ethical questions for which clear answers are difficult to answer. The APA Ethical Principles of Psychologists and Code of Conduct (American Psychological Association, 2010) in the Avoiding Harm Standard 3.04 states "Psychologists take reasonable steps to avoid harming their employees/ patients, students, supervisees, research participants, organizational employees and others with whom they work, and to minimize harm where it is foreseeable and unavoidable" and the Assessment Standard 9.02a states "Psychologists administer, adapt, score, interpret or use assessment techniques, interviews, tests or instruments in a manner and for purposes that are appropriate in light of the research on or evidence of the usefulness and proper application of the techniques."

These ethical guidelines suggest that when open-ended comments are overwhelmingly negative with little prescriptive feedforward suggestions to improve, consultants should consider reasonable options to organize and summarize the themes of the feedback and present them back to the employee in a manner that will engender understanding, acceptance and the management of potential negative emotional reactions. The findings of Smither et al., (2004) highlight the necessity to minimally follow-up with employees after they have received and reviewed their 360-degree feedback report to ensure that any negative emotions and reactions can be processed in a healthy manner.

Like quantitative results, open-ended comments create strong emotional reactions that can interfere with the acceptance of feedback and lead to diminished engagement and performance.

Additional research on ways to improve gathering constructive and meaningful "feedforward" comments from raters and the impact of such ratings on employee's motivation, emotional reactions, and readiness to change future behavior would appear to be warranted.

34. *Should you edit or delete critical and non-helpful open-ended comments?*

Participants generally find comments from open-ended questions useful and a great way of clarifying the sometimes confusing quantitative scores (e.g., when rater agreement is low but average scores are moderate or moderately high). Open-ended comments do have some potential downsides, as they take more time to complete and require more effort on the part of raters to make them more behavioral and useful. Open-ended comments might also reveal the raters, diminishing anonymity in the feedback process.

Some vendors may decide to remove critical comments to minimize potentially negative reactions, and others believe they have an unwritten contract with raters to allow them to share any recommendations, suggestions, and observations they have as part of the 360-degree process. Some vendors might also build in the capacity to correct spelling of rater comments and allow for multiple languages to be collected (Envisia Learning, Inc. has this feature in its customized 360 engine).

The determination of what constitutes "non-helpful" comments is challenging for those arguing that highly critical, judgmental, or hurtful comments should be eliminated before the report is shared with the participant. Most consultants follow ethical guidelines that value not harming participants emotionally in some way with the feedback interventions they are using. However, the decision to remove or delete potentially hurtful comments might be a decision that is left at the coach or consultant level and not one that a vendor should ever be involved in deciding. If the feedback to a participant is quite negative, finding a way to deliver the message in a way that minimizes defensiveness and emotional pain while enhancing acceptance can be quite challenging for most HR practitioners.

35. *Does a 360-degree feedback report require debriefing?*

"Best practices" in 360-degree feedback processes suggest that greater transfer of learning and goal setting occurs when a manager and/or coach helps employees understand and debrief their reports (Nowack, 2009). For example, Arthur, Bennett, Stanush, and McNelly (1998) conducted a meta-analysis of knowledge and skill decay studies and reported that one day after training, trainees exhibit little to no skill decay, but one year after training they lost over 90% of what they learned. Some vendors and some consultants espouse the *"diagnose and adios"* approach to 360-degree feedback, hoping that self-directed reflection alone will result in motivated behavioral change efforts.

In one of the few prospective empirical studies conducted on the impact of executive coaching, Smither, et al., (2003) reported that after receiving 360-degree feedback, managers who worked with a coach were significantly more likely to set measureable and specific goals and solicit ideas for improvement. They subsequently received significantly improved performance ratings. Thatch (2002) found that in six weeks of executive coaching following 360-degree feedback, performance increased by 60 percent.

In a much cited study in the public sector, Olivero, Bane, and Kopelman (1997) found that employee feedback and coaching for two-months increased productivity above the effects of a managerial training program (22.4 versus 80.0 percent) for 31 employees. These coaching studies support the importance of supportive follow-up after feedback is received to facilitate developmental action planning and the practice of targeted behaviors.

Some limited support for other approaches to structured follow-up comes from a recent doctoral dissertation study evaluating the effectiveness of 360-degree feedback interventions in 257 leaders in diverse organizations (Rehbine, 2007). In this study, over 65 percent of those surveyed expressed a strong interest in utilizing some type of an online follow-up tool to measure progress and facilitate their own individual behavioral change efforts. However, newer research also suggests that the approach to coaching might be as important as the modality (self-directed using an online development and reminder system or coach directed).

A study by Hooijberg and Lane (2009) surveyed 232 managers from diverse organizations and investigated what makes coaching most effective for employees. One of the key questions asked was: "What did your coach do that you found most effective?" From the view of the employee or employees, three major categories determined feedback success: 1) interpreting results (34.8 percent), 2) inspiring action (27.5 percent), and 3) professionalism of the coach (23.3 percent). The majority of employees thought the best consultants were those who analyzed strengths and weaknesses, helped assimilate feedback, and made concrete developmental recommendations.

This study seems to contradict much of the coaching literature and suggests that employees using 360-degree feedback expect and want their coach to take a much more active and directive role in interpreting their results and making developmental recommendations to leverage actual behavior change.

Overall, "best practices" would strongly suggest that 360-degree feedback reports be discussed with employees (or be made available with the use of highly structured online goal setting systems that are sometimes integrated with such feedback assessments). Greater use of "prescriptive" and "feedforward" suggestions on the part of the coach, manager, or consultant debriefing the report would appear to maximize readiness to change and the targeting of specific behaviors to use more, less or differently to enhance overall performance.

Consultants should utilize some of the prescriptive suggestions from models of transfer of training that suggest that factors before, during and after feedback can positively influence the extent of transfer back to the job (Grossman & Salas, 2011). Finally, based on research suggesting the importance of personality factors in feedback processes, consultants should carefully consider the mediating effects of self-efficacy, mastery goal orientation, and motivation to transfer during their debriefings to leverage learning transfer (Chiaburu, Van Dam, & Hutchins, 2010).

36. Should an individual 360-degree feedback report contain a mix of graphs, charts, tables and responses to open-ended questions to maximize understanding?

Little research exists to provide definitive answers as to the best way to present 360-degree feedback results to facilitate acceptance and enhance readiness to change behavior. However, it is intuitive that employees have different learning styles, and some may prefer to favor the interpretation of either qualitative over quantitative presentations of results or vice-versa. One study that does give some insight about what presentation style might maximize the acceptability, understanding, and interpretation of 360-degree feedback results comes from Atwater and Brett (2003). These researchers compared several different report presentations to participants and concluded that:

a. Individuals appear to be significantly less positive and less motivated after receiving text feedback than after receiving numeric feedback.

b. Individuals appear to prefer numeric over qualitative scores and normative over relative comparisons of self and other ratings in 360-degree summary reports and find these useful for development purposes.

Unfortunately, practice has truly outstripped research in guiding developers of 360-feedback assessments to optimize report content and to organize the presentation of data to enhance understanding and acceptance of results without it being confusing or overwhelming. Most 360-degree feedback reports tend to have common sections including: 1) Comparison of self-other rating similarities/differences using bar, line, spider, and scatterplot graphs to illustrate these gaps and trends; 2) A list of most and least frequently observed or effective behaviors that summarize strengths and development opportunities; and 3) Open-ended question narrative responses about development opportunities or strengths to leverage.

It appears that "what the crowd does" is what is now commonly accepted in how 360-degree feedback reports are organized and presented in light of a paucity of evidence based practices to guide developers and consultants. Until more research has accumulated, the findings of Atwater and Brett (2003) would appear to support the more popular and common approaches being used today. Future research should also explore the delivery of reports as well as the type of content made available to employees given new technological opportunities to receive and view reports on personal computers, portable tablets, and smartphones either in self-directed or facilitated fashion by consultants or others (e.g., showing selected report components via video conferencing).

37. What should you do if raters don't agree on their ratings?

Current research suggests that rater agreement will indeed vary in 360-degree feedback assessments largely because feedback research shows that different rater sources provide unique, performance-relevant information (Nowack, 2009; Lance, Hoffman, Gentry & Barankik, 2008). Given these findings, vendors who do not provide a way for participants to evaluate within-rater agreement in feedback may increase the probability that average scores used in reports can be easily misinterpreted, particularly if they are used by consultants to help participants using 360-degree feedback assessment focus on specific competencies and behaviors for developmental planning purposes.

Participants should reflect on why specific behaviors might be perceived and experienced positively by some raters and negatively by others. A large discrepancy by raters often suggests a polarized perspective and one that might require additional information gathering to truly understand the meaning of within-rater differences on the 360-degree feedback behavior in question.

38. How should the 360-degree feedback data be collected?

Today, almost all 360-degree feedback is collected using online surveys (although handwritten assessments may still be required in special circumstances). Previous research (Smither, Walker & Yap, 2004) demonstrates the equivalence of handwritten and online assessments. However, it is also recommended, when possible, to supplement online surveys and assessments with selected interviews or focus groups to ensure a greater specificity and clarity of feedback responses.

39. *Should participants share their report with others?*

In most 360-degree feedback processes used for developmental purposes, the participant is the only person who gets to keep a copy of the individual summary feedback report. In some cases, the report might be made available to an internal or external coach the participant is working with or a trainer or facilitator who is conducting an organizational workshop. It is typical for talent management and succession planning purposes that a copy of the feedback report might also be made available to one's manager or the human resources department. Of course, a participant who has a good relationship with his or her manager and engages with the manager as a performance coach will be expected to openly share his or her feedback report, whether formally part of a 360-degree feedback intervention or not.

40. *Do you need an external coach to debrief and interpret 360-degree feedback reports?*

"Best practices" in using 360-degree feedback suggest that having *someone* debrief the report is important to manage potential negative emotions surrounding the data, increase the understanding of rater differences, and facilitate developmental planning (Nowack, 2005). However, the process of discussing feedback results appears to be more important than *who* facilitates the discussion assuming the manager, coach, or employee has an understanding of the 360-degree feedback assessment, the competencies being measured, and basic helping skills.

Sometimes, having managers facilitate discussion of the results can have a distinct advantage in helping translate insight into developmental planning to support job performance and career growth (Rehbine, 2007).

41. *Can 360-degree feedback be used alongside personality and style assessments?*

In general, 360-degree feedback assessments provide data on how participants are perceived by others, while personality and style assessments provide insights about *why* people might behave as they do. Including a personality-and-style-based tool along with a 360-degree feedback assessment is common for many coaches, consultants, and organizations involved in leadership and talent management training or development interventions. Most consultants have their own favorite personality-and-style-based tools as part of their coaching toolkit. Together, these two types of assessments can help facilitate a deeper awareness, an understanding of the participant's strengths that can be leveraged, and blind spots to focus on for further development.

42. *What is a typical 360-degree feedback project time schedule?*

Most 360-degree feedback processes share a common timeline. The recommended process below will give you an idea of how long each step in a complete 360-degree feedback process might take, although it is highly dependent on the company culture, the purpose of the 360-degree intervention, and the availability of raters.

- Communication of 360-degree feedback process (one to two weeks, if in-house meetings are conducted with participants, invited raters, and managers)

- Selecting raters (one to two weeks, if participants discuss their rater pool with their manager)
- Distribution of online questionnaires (one to two weeks)
- Completion of online questionnaires (two to four weeks, but this depends on the nature of the project and organization)
- Processing of 360-degree feedback reports (one to two days)
- Feedback meetings (one two hours for each participant)
- Completion of development plan (one to two weeks)
- Reassessment (12-24 months)

43. *Should new employees be included in the 360-degree feedback process?*

The goal of 360-degree feedback is to provide useful, accurate, and constructive information to employees to leverage their strengths and focus on potential development areas. If employees are too new to a job role or organization, then raters are unlikely to have enough opportunity for specific feedback. Depending on the purpose of the 360-degree feedback intervention and the competency model being used, care should be taken if including employees with less than six months' tenure in a role or position in a 360-degree feedback process.

Most vendors provide "not applicable" or "unable to observe" as options on their typical response rating scale, so if a relatively new employee is included in a 360-degree feedback initiative, raters who don't have opportunities to observe the employee and provide useful feedback can utilize these response choices.

In such cases, the use of *open-ended* comments might be more useful for the initial impressions created by new employees to solicit and analyze or to help target important competencies and behaviors for developmental purposes.

44. *Should participants inform respondents that they have been invited to give feedback?*

In general, it is highly recommended that participants communicate to those they invite to be raters about the nature of the 360-degree initiative they are participating in, how the data will be used, what specific feedback would be most useful to the participants, and when they would like the feedback to be completed. Communication about the purpose of the 360-degree feedback assessment process and confidentiality with invited raters is likely to increase compliance and cooperation and reduce rater bias, especially if the participant is specific about the type of feedback that would be most helpful to him or her.

45. *How can employee development be facilitated?*

Multi-rater or 360-degree feedback systems that have an action plan linked to them have been shown to be more successful than those that do not. "Best practices" suggest that program participants and their managers should meet to discuss results and to implement a development plan for behavior change (Nowack, 2009; Nowack & Mashihi, 2012). This professional development plan should be included as part of the ongoing evaluation system to ensure that it is monitored and reviewed.

Note that the feedback results should not be used as part of any overall evaluation rating or compensation decisions, only as one part of the developmental planning process).

The professional development plan should be specific about additional training, on-the-job activities, or developmental resources that the talent will focus on.

Finally, it is recommended that the professional action plan be written and implemented using a current Web-based goal planning and evaluation system (e.g., using the online goal setting and evaluation coaching system called *Momentor* available through Envisia Learning, Inc.) to facilitate monitoring and tracking progress by an internal or external coach.

Figure 5-5

Interpreting / Leveraging

46. When are average scores in a 360-degree feedback report possibly misleading?
47. Should reports use normative scoring or relative (average) scoring?
48. What is the best standardized scoring to use (e.g., z-scores, t-scores)?
49. How can you measure whether raters agree with each other in completing 360-degree feedback assessments?
50. Which rater group should participants focus on for development?
51. Under what conditions does 360-degree feedback work best?
52. How often should you repeat a 360-degree feedback process?
53. How can the role of the manager help to leverage the impact of a 360-degree feedback intervention?
54. Does personality impact how participants respond to feedback?
55. How do you manage the feedback of participants who underestimate or overestimate their results?
56. How do you evaluate the impact of a 360-degree feedback project?
57. Are raters providing unique feedback to participants?
58. Which participants are most motivated to accept feedback and change behavior?
59. What kind of training or certification by consultants is recommended to help participants understand and interpret their 360-degree feedback?
60. Are there cultural differences to be considered in the use of 360-degree feedback?
61. How many development goals should be included to maximize successful behavior change?
62. What are the advantages of "mini pulse surveys" to mea-sure ongoing progress in behavior change efforts?
63. How can you leverage the impact of impact of 360-degree feedback to ensure successful behavior change?

INTERPRETING AND LEVERAGING IMPACT

46. *When are average scores within 360-degree feedback reports misleading?*

Average scores are typically used by vendors in 360-degree feedback reports. However, without a way to discern outliers, polarized scores and rater agreement, the interpretation of average scores can be quite misleading in reports. For example, if a vendor provides a table of most and least frequent behaviors, it is not uncommon to use average scores to present these results. It is important that vendors provide a metric to determine whether these average scores reflect homogeneity of rater responses or enough dispersion to make the average score difficult to practically use for developmental planning efforts.

For example, in each of the 360-degree feedback reports produced by Envisia Learning, Inc., there is a section at the end that provides a summary table containing average competency and item scores by each rater group, as well as an overall average of all raters, excluding self-ratings. Each item or question measuring specific competencies is grouped under its appropriate competency to assist in the interpretation of the results. A feature of this section is the Index of Rater Agreement, shown in parentheses after the average scores for each rater group. This Index of Rater Agreement ranges from 0 to 1.0 and is based on a statistical measure of dispersion or spread by raters, called standard deviation. This index is derived by subtracting 1 from the calculated standard deviation divided by a scale-specific divisor.

An agreement index score of 0.0 suggests little or no rater agreement among those answering a specific question. An agreement score of 1.0 suggests uniform and consistent ratings by all raters providing feedback. Agreement index scores less than .50 might suggest a greater diversity, inconsistency, and spread among the raters.

It is not uncommon to misinterpret average scores represented on graphic comparisons as being accurate. However, when the *Index of Rater Agreement* is less than .50, it might suggest caution in interpreting these average scores. In reality, some raters might have a very positive bias in responding to the questions, whereas other raters might have a very negative bias in responding, creating a polarized view of the respondent. The *Rater Agreement Index* can be calculated at both the item and competency level. At the item level, it indicates the amount of rater agreement in answering each 360-degree feedback question.

47. *Should you use average or normative scoring in reports to facilitate interpretation?*

All vendors tend to aggregate results from different rater groups in 360-degree feedback reports in some manner to facilitate the interpretation, understanding, and acceptance of data. Most commonly, aggregate data is presented as *average* scores across all raters in a particular category. Average scores simply allow comparison of all raters within a category to self-assessment scores, based on mathematical calculations of the mean scores of the raters.

Some vendors also provide *normative*, or benchmark, scoring based, on global, industrial, or company-specific groups within a database that can be used for external or internal comparison. For example, Envisia Learning, Inc. has extensive North American, European, and global norms for all of its off-the-shelf validated 360-degree feedback assessments. Each year, the norm groups are analyzed and updated to ensure that they represent the most up-to-date benchmark. Additional details are also made available to characterize the norm group by gender, age, ethnicity, tenure, job level, and industry, so that greater understanding will occur if such norms are used within 360-degree feedback reports.

The use of norms in a 360-degree feedback report can be represented by several *standardized statistics* to enable the understanding of differences between self-perception and others' perception of the participant, relative to the specific norm group used. For example,

Envisia Learning, Inc., provides a choice of two standardized norm presentations that can be used in feedback reports: 1) z-scores (standardized score with a mean of 0 and standard deviation of 1) or 2) t-scores (standardized scores with a mean of 50 and standard deviation of 10).

Standardized t-scores are very common in psychological assessments. They standardize the mean to be 50 and the standard deviation to be 10 (approximately 68 percent of everyone in the database will have t-scores between one standard deviation above and below the mean). Standardized z-scores are less common in psychological assessments. They standardize the mean to be 0.0 and the standard deviation to be 1 (approximately 68 percent of everyone in the database will have a z-score between one standard deviation above and below the mean). In Envisia Learning, Inc., reports using standardized scores, we will also present the *percentile* equivalent score at the bottom of both graphs.

The use of norms in 360-degree feedback reports should not be taken lightly as a report preference, despite the size or representation of the norm group being used. In some cases, simple average score comparisons are best to help facilitate the understanding of self-other differences. In other cases, having an internal or external normative benchmark might be useful and desirable in comparing how self-others differences compare to these normative groups.

48. *What is the best standardized score to use?*

Some coaches, consultants, and organizations might prefer to use one type of standardized score over another in feedback reports. For example, z-scores often result in scores that are *negative* if they are below the mean, which could create an emotional reaction on the part of participants interpreting their results. It is important to keep in mind that all standardized scores (e.g., sten scores, percentiles, t-scores, z-scores) are representing the same data to the participant. However, some might be easier to interpret and understand. Organizations should use vendors that provide for the same flexibility in the use of standardized scores within 360-degree feedback reports as we do at Envisia Learning, Inc., to maximize acceptance and understanding.

49. *How can you measure if raters agree with each other?*

Dispersion, agreement, or variance *within* rater groups is important to measure and report back to participants in 360-degree feedback reports (Nowack, 2009). At Envisia Learning, Inc., we provide up to three *different* types of metrics of rater agreement within each of our reports including:

- The range of scores (indicates a band of responses, from the highest to lowest scores on a specific competency by all raters)
- The distribution of scores (indicates a visual way to discern the *spread* of scores by raters on specific questions)
- The statistical measure of rater agreement, based on standard deviation from 100 percent agreement to no agreement; any agreement *less than 50 percent* statistically is meaningful and

indicates enough variability within raters to suggest that the average score could be misleading if used to highlight strengths or potential development areas.

50. *Which rater group should you focus on for development?*

Differences between raters on 360-degree feedback assessments are common, and research suggests that the different rater groups are often only moderately associated with each other (Nowack, 1992). However, these meaningful rater group differences might also be a point of confusion in the interpretation of data for participants trying to use the results to determine specific behaviors to modify and which stakeholder to target.

At a practical level, this means that participants might be challenged to understand how to interpret observed differences by rater groups and asked whether to decide to focus their developmental "energy" on managing upward, downward, or laterally in light of these potentially discrepant results. Research suggests that raters tend to use specific *filters* when completing 360-degree feedback assessments (Nowack, 2009; Nowack & Mashihi, 2012). For example, superiors tend to focus more on performance, output, and task-oriented behaviors (Nowack, 2002).

In our research, we find that managers tend to reflect on three things when they complete 360-degree feedback assessments: 1) bottom-line performance (does the employee meet or exceed his or her performance objectives?), 2) technical competence (does the employee technically know what he or she is doing?), and 3) "burr in the saddle effect" (has the employee created situations or problems that require the manager to investigate further or try to spend time resolving internal or external customer complaints?). Employees who are viewed by managers as getting work done with quality, as possessing strong technical competence, and as minimizing extra work on the part of the manager to resolve internal or external political issues are generally rated higher on 360-degree feedback assessments.

In general, direct reports tend to emphasize and filter *interpersonal and relationship* behaviors into their subjective ratings, whereas peers tend to be fairly accurate in actually predicting future leadership potential (although it is unclear exactly what qualities, competencies, personality attributes, or other behaviors they might be weighing when they complete 360-degree assessments). Based on these rating filters,

observational opportunities, and job-role relationships with participants, it seems that peer ratings might be interpreted as an important message about *moving ahead*, whereas direct report ratings might be interpreted as an important message about *getting along*. Participants should consider both the source and the congruence between various rater groups in determining which one they might target as a part of their developmental planning.

51. *Under what conditions does 360-degree feedback work best?*

Generally, 360-degree feedback processes, in order to be effective, depend on the participant, the coach, and organizational factors to support the receptivity, acceptance, and leveraging of feedback for enhanced insight and behavioral change. Several studies by Envisia Learning, Inc., have suggested some "Best Practices" that should be followed including those outlined below (Nowack, 2005; 2009). When the organizational culture is conducive to giving and receiving feedback and not under some major change effort, the implementation of a

360-degree feedback intervention is most likely to be met with success that is consistent with its goals.

1. Define and communicate clearly about the purpose of the 360-degree feedback intervention, including the limits of confidentiality and anonymity

2. Provide individual coaching to assist in interpreting and using the 360-degree feedback results

3. Hold the participant and manager accountable to create and implement a professional development plan

4. Track and monitor progress on the completion of the development plan

5. Link the 360-degree feedback intervention to a human resources performance management process

6. Use 360-degree feedback assessments with sound psychometric properties

7. Target competencies for 360-degree feedback interventions that are related to strategic business needs

52. *How often should you repeat a 360-degree feedback process?*

Given that people need time to make meaningful behavioral change and then time for that change to be seen by others, we recommend that somewhere between 12 to 24 month intervals are most appropriate for repeating a 360-degree feedback process. This allows people to work through their development and action plans to create change. For example, Envisia Learning Inc. provides a *time series 360-degree feedback report* that combines and summarizes results from the first and subsequent administrations of 360-degree feedback to show change in scores over a time period. Of course, it is also highly recommended to periodically evaluate the impact of the participant's goal setting and development plan progress. Envisia Learning has a goal evaluation system within its goal setting platform called Momentor which can be administered at any time following coaching or training that asks invited raters to evaluate progress on specific participant goals. This feedback is combined into a brief report to help provide accountability and measure learning transfer.

53. *How can the role of the manager help to leverage the impact of 360-degree feedback to ensure successful behavioral change?*

Organizations that implement a systemic approach to talent development with support from a manager and follow up development activities tied to performance improvement will have the most effective outcomes in leadership development (Nowack, 2009). A better understanding of the role of the manager as an important internal coach and how organizational culture influences promoting and sustaining new behavior is in need of greater exploration. The manager can reinforce and support the implementation of the development plan of the participant. This is important in light of recent findings suggesting that effect sizes for transfer of management training interventions are generally low (particularly when seen by direct reports and peers) but can be improved significantly with opportunities for structured and deliberate practice (Taylor, Taylor, & Russ-Eft, 2009).

Use of newer online goal setting and development planning/ reminder systems like *Momentor* by Envisia Learning, Inc. (https:// www.envisialearning.com/momentor) and follow-up in order to leverage multi-rater feedback interventions. In a recent unpublished one-year longitudinal study using this online coaching system with a major university medical center, significant behavioral change was observed by managers, direct reports, and peers on a post-program assessment (Nowack, 2011). This finding suggests that performance can be practically enhanced by using a 360-degree feedback process involving managers as "performance coaches" and holding participants accountable for creating and implementing a development plan based on 360 results.

54. *Does personality impact how people respond to 360-degree feedback?*

Personality appears to directly influence how employees react to 360-degree feedback, how motivated they will be to act on the observations and suggestions of others, and how likely they will be to implement and sustain new behaviors to become more effective. For example, research by Smither, London, and Richmond (2005) explored the relationship between personalities of leaders and their reactions to and use of 360-degree feedback. Leaders high in the five-factor personality facet of emotional stability were significantly more likely to be rated by a psychologist as motivated to use the feedback results for their ongoing professional development. Additionally, leaders high in extraversion were significantly more likely to have sought additional feedback six months later, while leaders high in conscientiousness were more likely to have actually engaged in developmental behaviors. These researchers and others have found that extraverted leaders who were also high on the personality factor of openness to experience were more likely to perceive and view negative feedback as valuable data and were most likely to seek further information about their feedback (Bell & Arthur, 2008). Several studies support the findings that individuals with high self-esteem report more favorable attitudes toward the 360-degree feedback results than those with low self-esteem (Bono & Colbert, 2005). Feedback recipients who rated themselves highly on receptivity and the desire to make a good first impression were also perceived by feedback providers as having more positive reactions to feedback (Atwater, Brett, & Charles, 2007) as well as employees who generally rated themselves lower than others (Brett & Atwater, 2001).

Research by Bono and Colbert (2005) provided evidence that the motivation to change behavior following 360-degree feedback is related to a meta-personality concept called core self-evaluations (CSE). Specifically, they found that individuals with high levels of core self-evaluations (those with high self-esteem, generalized self-efficacy, internal locus of control and low neuroticism) will be most motivated to initiate change behavior when they receive discrepant feedback, while those with low levels of core self-evaluations will be most motivated when others' ratings are most similar to their own. As such, the personality of the employee has a direct result in the level of readiness to change based on both the direction and magnitude of self-other agreement.

The stable personality trait of goal orientation has also been shown to influence whether an individual views feedback as a development opportunity or a challenge to his or her self-rating (Dweck, 1986). Individuals with a learning goal orientation tend to hold a view of ability as modifiable and believe they are capable of improving their level of abilities (Brett & Atwater, 2001). These researchers found that those with a learning goal orientation believed the feedback was more usefulthan those with a performance goal orientation.

Taken together, it seems employees are most motivated to use 360-degree feedback for development when they are conscientious, achievement oriented, extraverted, possess high self-efficacy, have an internal locus of control, a learning goal orientation, and express low anxiety. Identifying and understanding the personality of employees will help consultants to structure coaching and feedback interventions in a manner that facilitates both readiness to change and the enhancement of self-efficacy (Rhodes, Plotnikoff, & Courneya, 2009).

Consultants might also consider including a newer generation five-factor personality inventory or a structured interview in their practice to assess personality factors that might contribute or hinder to the acceptance of 360-degree feedback and overall commitment to initiate and sustain successful behavior change over time. For example, employees who report being low on conscientiousness tend to be less capable of controlling, regulating, and directing their impulses and, as such, may be less committed to long-term behavior change and personal/ professional development (Klockner & Hicks, 2008). In such cases, consultants may need to explore ways to structure behavior change efforts to maximize recognition and reinforcement after short-term goal accomplishments and schedule structured follow-up with their employees using a variety of methods (e.g., meetings, email reminders) to encourage continued efforts.

55. *How do you manage the feedback of underestimators and overestimators?*

It has been estimated that 65 to 75 percent of the employees in any given organization report that the worst aspect of their job is their immediate boss (Hogan, 2007, p. 106). In fact, estimates of the base rate for managerial incompetence in organizations range from 30 to 75 percent, with the average level of poor leadership estimated at about 50 percent (Hogan & Kaiser, 2005). Many of these incompetent leaders tend to have inflated views of their skills and abilities, and this appears fairly common in 360-degree feedback research (Atwater & Brett, 2005). In a study by Vecchio and Anderson (2009), the tendency to overestimate one's own leader effectiveness relative to evaluations provided by others was found to be greater for males and older managers.

These self-enhancers or overestimators are often blind to accurately identifying their own strengths, less receptive to feedback from others, have negative reactions to feedback (Brett and Atwater, 2001), and are at high risk for derailment (Quast, Center, Chung, Wohkittel, & Vue, 2011). As a result, consultants might find it difficult to find the "what's in it for me" with such employees to accept the perceptions of others and commit to modifying their behavior to some degree in order to better meet the expectations and needs of those working with them.

In a Harvard Business Review article, Kaplan and Kaiser (2009) argue that it is just as detrimental to overuse our strengths as it is to underuse them. In their research, those expressing the right amount of strength showed a significant association with a measure of leadership success. As the authors point out, leveraging and emphasizing strength might lead to actually interfering with being flexible and adopting new behaviors.

Goffin and Anderson (2007) found in their study of 204 managers that self-rating inflation was significantly correlated with high achievement, self-esteem, and social desirability personality factors. This personality profile pattern suggests that self-enhancers might possess an exaggerated perception of their strengths result in in potential defensiveness and resistance during 360-degreee feedback discussions with their coach or others.

It should also be noted that the pattern of high social desirability and low anxiety (repressive coping) has long been shown in the health psychology literature to be significantly associated with increased cardiovascular reactivity to stress, higher blood pressure, and poor overall health outcomes (Mund & Mitte, 2011; Rutledge, 2006).

This pattern, found in an earlier Goffin and Anderson (2002) study, suggests that overestimators might not only be at risk to derail in their careers but also vulnerable to negative physical health outcomes. To date, no research has directly tested this hypothesis or considered that the most vulnerable overestimator might indeed be a personality profile characterized as high in social desirability, low in negative affect (anxiety), and simultaneously high in positive affect (i.e., a "super repressor").

Another form of "cognitive distortion" that is common in 360-degree feedback processes are characterized by employees rating themselves significantly lower than the ratings of others. These underestimators are actually viewed as possessing strengths but not fully recognizing or acknowledging them relative to others giving them feedback (Nowack, 2009). Furthermore, research by Goffin and Anderson (2007) suggests that underestimators score significantly higher on negative affect than overestimators, suggesting they are likely to be more emotionally reactive, anxious, and nervous in the interpretation of their feedback results. Nowack (2009) reported that underestimators (about 25 to 30 percent of those taking 360-degree assessments) are typically characterized as highly perfectionist, expect high performance for themselves and others, focus on their weaknesses and look for fault, criticism, and potential deficits in their feedback from others, and reframe feedback suggesting strengths as being too complimentary.

In summary, underestimators tend to minimize the strengths seen by others and dwell on anything that isn't perfect in their summary feedback report. In practice, these employees are resistant to leverage their strengths as seen by others even when it is pointed out that they are underestimating how others are experiencing the frequency or effectiveness of their expressed behavior. The underestimators tend to be hyper-vigilant to anything they perceive to be critical or negative in 360-degree feedback reports and emphasize what they perceive to be developmental opportunities or weaknesses.

Consultants should become familiar with the impact of employee self-enhancement (both magnitude and direction) on the understanding, acceptance, and actions taken following 360-degree feedback as well as how it might predict job performance (Nowack & Mashihi, 2012). For example, a study by Atwater et al., (1998) found that leadership effectiveness in 1,460 managers was highest when both self and other ratings were high, and when self-ratings were substantially lower than other ratings (severe underestimation). Effectiveness was the lowest for overestimators when self-rating was only moderate and subordinate ratings were low.

The discrepancy between self-ratings and other ratings can affect both emotional reactions and readiness to change behavior. Current research suggests mixed findings for the association between affect and behavioral change. For example, Atwater and Brett (2005) suggest that leaders who received low ratings and overrated themselves were actually more motivated to change than leaders who received low ratings and gave themselves low ratings. However, these over-raters also had more negative reactions (e.g., were more angry) than those who did not overrate. In contrast, other research suggests that overestimators are significantly less likely to engage in developmental plans following negative feedback (Woo, Sims, Rupp, & Gibbons, 2008).

Consultants should be aware that employees who are underestimators are likely to be highly perfectionistic, self-critical, and express high negative affect making them likely to dismiss the strengths perceived by others. It should be expected that underestimating employees will not see their feedback in balance and consultants should anticipate that their employees will accentuate and focus on the negative, despite feedback from others that they are actually performing strongly or possess high competence in particular skills and abilities being rated. In practice, getting underestimating employees to leverage their strengths in developmental planning is one of the biggest challenges faced by consultants during 360-degree feedback meetings.

In contrast, employees who are overestimators are likely to be highly achievement oriented, express high self-esteem, project a socially desirable impression of their behaviors, and report little anxiety. Consultants should also note that self-enhancing assessments of poor performance ratings from others may take different forms such as attending selectively to only the positive indicators or minimizing negative indicators. Jordan and Audia (2012) point out three common self-enhancing assessments of receiving low performance ratings from others including: 1) Downplaying the importance of the performance goals to perceive low performance in a more positive light; 2) Redefining the level of abstraction of a performance goal to make it more flexible or broad; and 3) Focusing on how things could have been worse if they had acted differently (i.e., focusing on counterfactual outcomes as comparisons).

In practical terms, sometimes consultants have to work hard to "find the crease" to allow employees to digest and accept constructive negative feedback they have received without dismissing it outright. Finally, it is important to note that people not only compare themselves to others, but also how they used to be in the past. In general, individuals evaluate their current and future selves as better than their past selves (Wilson & Ross, 2001), suggesting that consultants should focus their developmental planning efforts with employees in a future-oriented manner and help them compare one's "ideal self" to one's "real self" (Boyatzis & Akrivou, 2006).

56. How do you evaluate the impact of 360-degree feedback?

The initial 360-degree feedback provides a benchmark and baseline for the talent. It is hoped that the results of the 360-degree feedback program will result in enhanced performance and effectiveness. One important metric in evaluating this type of training intervention is to compare change over time on the key competencies being measured through the 360-degree feedback assessment. This ensures that the 360-degree feedback process focuses on individual change, rather than being a one-time event. This is frequently seen within many organizations.

"Best Practices" suggest that the 360-degree feedback process be repeated 12 to 24 months following the initial administration of feedback to facilitate the effectiveness of the training program and monitor individual progress on individual development plans (Nowack, 2005; 2009; Nowack, Hartley, & Bradley, 1999). Surveys and focus groups can also be used to evaluate the 360-degree feedback process to help determine what things can be changed for future organizational interventions and projects.

57. Are raters providing unique feedback?

As mentioned earlier, different raters do appear to be applying different observational filters that bias and reflect on the behaviors they are rating (Nowack, 2009; Nowack & Mashihi, 2012). As such, ratings from managers appear to be performance-oriented, ratings from direct reports are more interpersonally oriented, and ratings from peers are focused on future leadership potential.

At a practical level, this suggests that results from 360-degree feedback do prompt unique feedback from the different rater groups involved in such processes. As such, each rater group provides important but somewhat unique feedback to interpret and decide how to use in each 360-degree feedback process.

58. *Which participants are most motivated to accept feedback?*

Limited research suggests that two factors play a role in who is most likely to be the most motivated and respond the most favorably to 360-degree feedback (Atwater & Brett, 2006). The findings suggest that:

- Individuals who have higher levels of organizational commitment are more motivated to change, regardless of the nature of the feedback.
- Individuals who hold more positive attitudes toward the feedback process are also more motivated to change and report more follow-up activities than those who held less positive attitudes.

Smither, Brett, and Atwater (2008) examined some of the factors that influence the accessibility of feedback and subsequent improvement in performance. First, participants are more likely to recall positive, rather than negative, feedback from others. Second, participants are more inclined to recall feedback that relates to their performance orientation but not as likely to recall feedback that concerns their capacity to develop subordinates. Third, participants were more inclined to recall feedback that alluded to specific, tangible behaviors, rather than global, abstract traits. Finally, participants were more likely to recall feedback from supervisors and subordinates than from peers.

59. What kind of training or certification by consultants is required to help employees understand and interpret 360-degree feedback reports?

HR practitioners may have very diverse backgrounds and academic degrees, but familiarity with assessments in general should be required to professionally utilize 360-degree feedback systems (Nowack, 2003). In their article in *Harvard Business Review*, Sherman and Freas (2004) stated that executive coaching is "Like the Wild West of yesteryear, this frontier (executive coaching) is chaotic, largely unexplored, and fraught with risk, yet immensely promising" (pp. 82-83).

Current research on coaching differences by education and training has found that psychologists are more likely to meet face-to-face, contract for fewer sessions, and are more likely to use 360-degree assessments in their practice than non-psychologists (Bono, et al., 2009). Bono et al., (2009) found in their study of 428 consultants (256 non-psychologists, 172 psychologists) that differences were generally small (average difference= .26) and there were as many differences between psychologists in their training and orientation to coaching (e.g., clinical, social/personality or industrial/ organizational) as between consultants and non-psychologists.

Additionally, these researchers reported that psychologist coaches were "more likely to use effective tools to diagnose the problem (e.g., multisource behavioral ratings, interview with a supervisor, and interview with peers, ability/aptitude tests, and review of prior performance data" (p. 390).

Consultants should be knowledgeable and competent in the use and interpretation of assessments including 360-degree feedback. In light of current research, it would appear necessary that consultants possess adequate measurement and statistical expertise to fully explain and interpret 360-degree feedback results to their employees.

Consultants should continue to pursue continuing education and training to enhance their knowledge (e.g., use of assessments), skills (e.g., managing tricky ethical dilemmas), and abilities (handling resistance) to help their employees gain self-insight and facilitate long-term behavioral change success. For example, if an executive coach is clinically trained as a psychologist he or she might need to enhance their knowledge about business/industry, or if trained in a research oriented industrial-organizational psychology program, he or she might need to enhance core counseling skills.

60. Are there cultural differences to be considered in the use of 360-degree feedback?

There is increasing use of 360-degree feedback in different cultures and countries, as multi-national companies utilize it throughout their entire organization. Differences in 360-degree feedback rating and interpretation should be expected to some degree in other cultures. Several cultural dimensions have been thoroughly studied (Hofstede & McRae, 2004) and would appear to be meaningful to 360-degree ratings (self and others). These cultural dimensions include individualism versus collectivism, power distance, uncertainty avoidance, short- term versus long-term orientation, and gender egalitarianism.

Varela and Premeaux (2008), in their sampling of managers in Latin America, found the least discrepancy between peer and self-ratings. In their analysis, direct reports gave the highest ratings to their managers in this highly collectivistic and high power distance culture. Cultural differences between geographic regions in Asia have been found to be associated with patterns of self-ratings of managerial performance (Gentry, Yip, & Hannum, 2010). These researchers found those significant self-other discrepancies were wider in high power and individualistic cultures mainly due to the subject's self-ratings and not the ratings of others. In a comparison of U.S. managers (N=22, 362) to an Asian sample of 3,810 managers consisting of five countries, Quast et al., (2011) found that self-other discrepancies in all countries were significantly associated with bosses' predictions of how likely a manager was to experience future career derailment. These results provide support for earlier findings that self-other rating discrepancies are associated with derailment in the U.S and extend these findings to the five Asian countries included in this study (China, S. Korea, Japan, India, and Thailand).

Atwater, Wang, Smither, and Fleenor (2009) explored self and subordinate ratings of leadership in 964 managers from 21 countries, based on assertiveness, power distance, and individualism or collectivism. Self and other ratings were more positive in countries characterized as high in both assertiveness and power distance. However, Atwater, et al., (2005) found varying multi-source ratings patterns (i.e., self-other agreement) in different cultures. Their study showed that links between self-other discrepancies and managerial effectiveness varied greatly and these discrepancies were related to effectiveness in the US but not in the European and Scandinavian countries of Germany, Denmark, Italy, and France (only others' ratings of leadership predicted managerial effectiveness.

In one of the broadest studies to date, Eckert, Ekelund, Gentry, and Dawson (2010) investigated self-observer rating discrepancies on three leadership skills on data from 31 countries. They reported that rater discrepancy on a manager's decisiveness and composure was higher in high power distance cultures (e.g. Asian) than low power distance cultures (e.g. Americas). Self–observer rating discrepancy has also been shown to be higher (i.e., bigger or wider) for U.S. American managers than for Europeans on 360-degree ratings of managerial derailment behaviors (Gentry, Hannum, Ekelund, & de Jong, 2007). At least in the U.S., higher disagreement between self and observer ratings is generally associated with lower effectiveness and job performance (Ostroff, Atwater, & Feinberg, 2004; Atwater & Brett, 2005), but some contradictory evidence has been found in other countries (Atwater, et al., 2009).

Cultural relevance was compared across five countries (US, Ireland, Israel, Philippines, and Malaysia) and this supported the overall effectiveness of the 360-degree feedback process but also revealed important differences (Shipper, Hoffman, & Rotondo, 2007). This study suggested that the 360-degree feedback process is relevant in all cultures but most effective in those low on power distance with individualistic values (e.g., United States versus Philippines). Finally, earlier research on 360-degree feedback across 17 countries by Robie, Kaster, Nilsen, and Hazucha (2000) suggested that there were more similarities than differences across countries. For example, the ability to solve complex problems and learn quickly appears to be universally predictive of effectiveness for leaders across cultures high and low in power.

In general, interpreting the current literature of 360-degree feedback across countries and cultures is somewhat difficult given the different competencies being evaluated in the studies cited (the majority were vendor developed), the various approaches to measuring self-other differences (from simple algebraic difference scores to uses of more sophisticated polynomial regression) and the diverse performance/ derailment outcome measures used (e.g., single item predictions of derailment to managerial performance ratings). Additional research is needed and will continue to guide consultants to understanding the cross-cultural implications surrounding the effective use of feedback interventions and the meaningfulness of the gaps between self and other differences.

Taken together, these newer cross-cultural 360-degree feedback studies suggest that factors such as values, norms, and beliefs have an impact on self–other rating discrepancies and their meaning. Despite some contradictory evidence, the relevance of self-other ratings appears to be important for consultants to use and interpret for both development and non-development purposes and appears to impact both leadership performance and potential derailment. In general, peer ratings appear to have utility for predicting future leadership potential across cultures. Consultants who work with multi-national organizations should continue to develop their own cultural competence and knowledge of relevant norms, values, and history as they interact with leaders and talent at all levels.

Additionally, alternative competency models defining cross-cultural leaders might be strongly considered for future feedback interventions given the lack of a universal taxonomy or systematic framework for evaluating the content coverage of such assessments (Holt et al., 2012). Current research suggests that many 360-degree feedback assessments with multiple competencies lack research-based frameworks, are often highly intercorrelated with each other (Hoffman & Woehr, 2009), and typically possess a small number of underlying factors (Smither et al., 2005).

For example, consultants should be familiar with the research behind the competency framework used in the particular 360-degree feedback assessment they are using. They should also have some understanding of the academic debate about various leadership taxonomies such as the "Great 8 Competencies" by Bartram (2005), the four theoretically derived behavioral types of leadership based on the extension of the transactional-transformational model of leadership by Pearce, Sims, Cox, Ball, Schnell, Smith, and Trevino (2003), and the three meta-categories of task, relations, and change behavior introduced by Yukl, Gordon, and Taber (2002).

Consultants should critically examine the competency based framework behind the specific 360-degree feedback assessment they are using and align the model with the specific goals of the project and the job level of the employees they are working with. They should only utilize commercially based, or organizationally developed, assessments that have adequate psychometric properties (e.g., internal consistency reliability) and a factor structure to support the breakdown of specific competencies that often are targeted for development planning by participants.

61. *How many goals should be included to maximize success in the development planning process?*

Behavioral change efforts are often not linear but tend to be progressive, regressive, or even static. It seems intuitive that focus on a single behavioral change goal is easier to initiate and sustain, but, surprisingly, multiple simultaneous efforts (e.g., behaviors planned to improve multiple competencies at the same time) tend to be equal or even more effective, because they reinforce quick benefits (Hyman, Pavlik, Taylor, Goodrick, & Moye, 2007). Of course, it is important for employees to be successful, so making sure that not too many unrealistic goals are set is something a coach can discuss with their employee. In our online coaching and goal-setting/evaluation system called Momentor, we allow participants to select as many competencies as they would like to begin their development plan.

At any point, they can add new goals and specific tasks, activities and actions to enhance their effectiveness.

62. *What are the advantages of "mini-surveys" to measure development progress?*

Tracking and monitoring progress on development plans is essential for sustaining new behavior over time. It is important to continuously seek feedback from others to see how a participant is progressing in their targeted goal. Research by Goldsmith (2006) on 8,208 leaders over an 18-month period shows the importance of follow-up with others (e.g., direct reports, peers and their managers):

- 53 percent of the leaders who did not follow-up were rated as unchanged or less effective

- 66 percent of the leaders who did "a little follow-up" showed improvement

- 95 percent of the leaders who did "a lot of follow-up" were rated as dramatically improved

Sometimes it is too early to conduct another full 360-degree feedback assessment or not feasible to do so. In such cases, the use of "mini-surveys" can be quite helpful in gathering quick feedback about whether others see employees improving, staying the same, or even getting worse on targeted competencies that have been a part of their development plan.

At Envisia Learning, Inc., we offer for each of our assessments a progress pulse *Goal Evaluation* within our development platform called Momentor that allows participants to gather information about their progress one or more of their developmental goals, using an effectiveness scale targeted to a specific competency. We allow participants to go out and solicit feedback from the original 360-degree rater pool or add new raters. These raters are simply asked to evaluate how effective the participant is on the competency being evaluated, as well as providing an open-ended comment to support the rating:

What changes do you notice in performance, effectiveness, and/ or behavior as it relates to the person's goal?

> *Worse*
> *No Change*
> *Improved*
> *Not Observed/Unable to Answer*

The results from the *Goal Evaluation* are summarized in a brief online report that provides a useful metric of effectiveness or improvement on the participant's developmental goals. Such feedback can be useful for additional development planning efforts.

63. *How can you leverage the impact of 360-degree feedback to ensure successful behavioral change?*

Smither, London, Flautt, Vargas, and Kucine (2003) found that leaders who received unfavorable feedback initially had negative reactions, but six months later they had created significantly more improvement goals than other leaders. They suggested "negative feedback may take a while to sink in or recipients may need some time to reflect and absorb the feedback" (p. 203) after the initial emotions have subsided. As pointed out earlier, Brett and Atwater (2001) found that individuals who received negative feedback from bosses and peers reported adverse emotional reactions. However, the impact of initial reactions seemed to lessen after several weeks, and was not related to perceived feedback usefulness despite the emotionality surrounding the process.

Taken together, these findings suggest two things. The first is that it is important to manage the initial emotional reactions that employees have and to identify key personality traits that might exacerbate or temper these responses (e.g., narcissism, self-esteem, and emotional stability). Second, translating awareness into goal implementations would appear to be most critical to ensure that employees translate the 360-degree feedback experience into deliberate practice of new behaviors to accentuate what they do well, acquire new habits or modify existing ones to become more effective (Nowack & Mashihi, 2012; Smither, Brett, & Atwater, 2008).

New evidence suggests that perceived importance of the desired behavioral change end-point is the best predictor differentiating non-intenders from those who are successful adopters of new behavior. However, self-efficacy, perceived control, and being clear about the "cons" behind behavioral change are more important in discriminating successful maintainers from unsuccessful maintainers who relapse and fall back to their older habits and routines (Rhodes, Plotnikoff, & Courneya, 2009).

Finally, recent research on goal accomplishment suggests that a shift in attention and motivation level from the starting point to the end point occurred halfway through the goal so this might be one of the most important times for consultants to follow-up with their employees and discuss possible relapse prevention strategies (Bonezzi, Brendl, & De Angelis, 2011). As such, employees might require more attention, reinforcement, and follow-up in the middle of a coaching intervention than any other time based on the course of motivation over time.

Developing expertise in complex activities undoubtedly requires deliberate practice (Ericcson, 2006; Nowack, 2015a) so that the new behavior is automatic (unconscious competence). However, it is likely that the popular myth of 10,000 hours of practice leading to expertise has research evidence to support this claim (Nowack, 2016b).

To investigate the process of habit formation in everyday life, 96 volunteers chose an eating, drinking, or activity behavior to carry out daily in the same context (for example "after breakfast") for 12 weeks. Participants completed a self-report tracking form each day and recorded whether they carried out the behavior (Lally, Van Haarsveld, Potts, & Wardle, 2010). The number of days it took for a new behavior to become "automatic" depended on its complexity (e.g., new eating habits 65 days and exercise 91 days). Of the 82 employees who saw the study through to the end, the most common pattern of habit formation was for early repetitions of the chosen behavior to produce the largest increases in its automaticity. Over time, further increases in automaticity dwindled until a plateau was reached beyond which extra repetitions made no practical difference to the automaticity achieved.

Organizations that implement a systemic approach to talent development with support from a manager and follow up development activities tied to performance improvement will have the most effective outcomes in leadership development (Nowack, 2009). A better understanding of the role of the manager as an important internal coach and how organizational culture influences promoting and sustaining new behavior is in need of greater exploration. The manager can play a big role to reinforce and support the implementation of the development plan of their direct report.

Use of newer online goal setting and development planning/ reminder systems may be promising and recent studies seem to suggest that employees are interested in using these for translating awareness from 360-degree feedback into behavior change (Rehbine, 2007). For example, in a recent unpublished one-year longitudinal study using an online goal setting and tracking system called Momentor with a major university medical center (Nowack, 2011), significant behavioral change was observed on an overall score averaged across all items and raters (managers, direct reports, and peers) on a post-program 360-feedback assessment $(F(2,11) = 4.72, p = .03)$.

Martin (2010) found a positive effect on learning transfer for peer support in a corporate field environment, with peer support and encouragement mitigating a negative work climate. Martin (2010) evaluated learning transfer on 237 managers of a manufacturing company in the Midwest U.S. who participated in a leadership development program. He found that leaders in a division with a more favorable climate and those reporting greater peer support showed the greatest transfer of learning but that support for peers bolstered transfer in the face of more negative work climates.

Additionally, managers who follow-up with talent who have taken 360-degree feedback assessments are more likely to set specific goals, solicit ideas for improvement, and subsequently receive improved performance ratings (Smither, London, Flautt, Vargas, & Kucine, 2003). These findings support the importance of involving the manager in the coaching intervention to leverage long-term behavior change success. This is important in light of recent findings suggesting that effect sizes for transfer of management training interventions are generally low (particularly when seen by direct reports and peers) but can be improved significantly with opportunities for structured and deliberate practice over time (Taylor, Taylor, & Russ-Eft, 2009).

Overall, these findings suggests that performance can be practically enhanced by using a 360-degree feedback process involving both peers as development partners and managers as performance consultants to hold employees accountable for creating and implementing a development plan based on 360-degree feedback results (Chiaburu & Marinova, 2005). Recent research suggests that stated goal intentions alone may not always result in successful maintenance of behavior over time (Lawton, Cooner, & McEachan, 2009). After 360-degree feedback, many employees express a strong desire and intent to become more effective and may actually try new behaviors. However, due to relapse these individuals might be unable to sustain them for very long. This suggests that consultants should emphasize relapse prevention techniques, facilitate self-efficacy, and become a "professional nag" to their employees to help reinforce new behavior change efforts (Rhodes, Plotnikoff, & Courneya, 2009). Consultants should also initially focus more on implementation intentions ("practice plans") with their employees using "if-then" goal statements to maximize behavioral change commitments, planning, and maintenance over time (Gollwitzer & Sheeran, 2009).

Summary

Enlightenment is about how individuals become aware of their strengths and weaknesses in order to develop. Assessing employees can involve a wide variety of approaches and tools, each with different predictors of future success and performance. HR practitioners should carefully consider what outcomes they are trying to achieve and select the assessment that best matches their goals. Multi-rater feedback systems are powerful and common tools for feedback and *must* be used with caution. If not, your employees' behavioral change can be more harmful than beneficial.

For example, employees often face the challenge of having views of themselves and their performance that are completely contrary to the views of their raters. For this reason, it is important for consultants to consider feedback tools that provide a theoretical foundation and are limited by reliability issues. Also, it is important for consultants and HR practitioners to be familiar with and use "Best Practices" when using 360-degree feedback interventions. The next section of the book provides exercises for all types of individuals who wish to increase self-insight and self-awareness.

Key Points

1. HR practitioners should understand the major assessment domains of skills and abilities, personality and style, interests and values, and health and well-being and what outcomes these domains are most strongly associated with in talent development.

2. Social and interpersonal stress causes the stress hormone to be elevated 50 percent longer, and social pain appears to use the same neurobiological pathways as physical pain.

3. The use of 360-degree feedback for the development of talent can be enhanced by following "Best Practices" in defining the purpose; designing and acquiring a psychometrically sound 360-degree feedback assessment; implementing a process to ensure confidentiality, trust, and anonymity; providing feedback in a manner that increases understanding and acceptance; and leveraging the feedback for successful behavioral change.

4. Keep in mind the *three tenets* of 360-degree feedback:

- *Feedback is important:* Most of us don't wake up each morning and spontaneously change behavior
- *You can't always get what you want*: Feedback doesn't always result in enhanced performance
- *Be realistic:* Don't expect 360-degree feedback to modify "competent jerks" into "lovable stars"

Enlighten References

3d Group (2013). *Current practices in 360-degree feedback: A benchmark study of North American Companies.* 3D Group. Berkeley, CA.

Ajzen, I. (1991). The theory of planned behaviour. *Organisational Behaviour and Human Decision Processes, 50,* 179–211.

American Psychological Association. (2010). American Psychological Association ethical principles of psychologists and code of conduct. Retrieved from http://www.apa.org/ethics/code/index.aspx#

Arthur, W., Jr., Bennett, W., Jr., Stanush, P. L., & McNelly, T. L. (1998). Factors that influence skill decay and retention: A quantitative review and analysis. *Human Performance, 11,* 57–101.

Arthur, W., Day, E. A., McNelly, T. & Edens, P. (2003). A meta-analysis of the criterion related validity of assessment center dimensions, *Personnel Psychology, 56,* 125-153.

Atwater, L., Ostroff, C., Yammarino, F. & Fleenor, J. (1998). Self-other agreement: Does it really matter? *Personnel Psychology, 51,* 577-598.

Atwater, L. A., Waldman, D., Atwater, D. & Cartier (2000). An upward feedback field experiment. Supervisors' cynicism, follow-up and commitment to subordinates. *Personnel Psychology, 53,* 275-297.

Atwater. L., Wang, M., Smither J. & Fleenor J. (2009). Are cultural characteristics associated with the relationship between self and others' ratings of leadership? *Journal of Applied Psychology, 94,* 876-886.

Atkins, P. W. B., & Wood, R. E. (2002). Self- versus others' ratings as predictors of assessment center ratings: Validation evidence for 360-degree feedback programs. *Personnel Psychology, 55,* 871-904.

Atwater, L. E., & Brett, J. F. (2005). Antecedents and consequences of reactions to developmental 360-degree feedback. *Journal of Vocational Behavior, 66,* 532–548.

Atwater, L. & Brett, J. (2006). 360-degree feedback to managers: Does it result in changes in employee attitudes? *Group & Organizational Management, 31*, 578-600.

Atwater, L., Brett, J., & Charles, A. (2007). Multi-source feedback: Lessons learned, and implications for practice. *Human Resource Management Journal, 46*, 285-307.

Atwater, L., Waldman, D., Ostroff, C., Robie, C., & Johnson, K. M. (2005). Self-other agreement: Comparing its relationship with performance in the U.S. and Europe. *International Journal of Selection and Assessment, 13*, 25-40.

Atwater, L.A., Waldman, D., Atwater, D., & Cartier, P. (2000). An upward feedback field experiment. Supervisors' cynicism, follow-up and commitment to subordinates. *Personnel Psychology, 53*, 275-297.

Atwater, L., Wang, M., Smither, J. & Fleenor, J. (2009). Are cultural characteristics associated with the relationship between self and others' rating of leadership? *Journal of Applied Psychology, 4*, 876-886.

Atwater, L., Brett, J. & Charles, A. (2007). Multisource feedback: Lessons learned and implications for practice. *Human Resource Management, 46*, 285-387.

Bandalos, D. L. & Enders, C. K. (1996). The effects of non-normality and number of response categories on reliability. *Applied Measurement in Education, 9*, 151-160.

Bandura, A. (1977). Self-Efficacy: Toward a unifying theory of behavior change. *Psychological Review, 84*, 191-215.

Bartram, D. (2005). The Great 8 competencies: a criterion-centric approach to validation. *Journal of Applied Psychology, 90*, 1185-1203.

Becker, M. H. (1974). The Health Belief Model and Personal Health Behaviour. *Health Education Monographs, 2*, 324-473.

Beehr, T. A., Ivanitskaya, L., Hansen, C. P., Erofeev, D., & Gudanowski, D. M. (2001). Evaluation of 360 degree feedback ratings: Relationships with each other and with performance and selection predictors. *Journal of Organizational Behavior, 22*, 775-788.

Belkic, K., Landsbergis, P., Schnall, P., Baker, D., Theiorell, T., Siegrist, J., Peter, R. & Karasek, R. (2000). Psychosocial factors: Review of the empirical data among men. Occupational Medicine: *State of the Art Reviews, 15*, 24-46.

Bell, S. T., & Arthur, W. A. (2008). Feedback acceptance in developmental assessment centers: the role of feedback message, participant personality, and affective response to the feedback session. *Journal of Organizational Behavior, 29*, 681–703.

Bonezzi A., Brendl, C. M., & De Angelis, M. (2011). Stuck in the middle: The psychophysics of goal pursuit. *Psychological Science, 22*, 607–612.

Bono, J. E., Purvanova, R. K., Towler, A. J. & Peterson, D. B. (2009). A Survey of Executive Coaching Practices. *Personnel Psychology, 62*, 361-404.

Bono, J. & Colbert, A. (2005). Understanding responses to multi-source feedback: The role of core self-evaluations. *Personnel Psychology, 58*, 171-203.

Borders, A., Jajodia, A. & Earleywine, M. (2010). Could mindfulness decrease anger, hostility, and aggression by decreasing rumination? *Aggressive Behavior, 36*, 28-44.

Boyatzis, R. E. (2008). Leadership development from a complexity perspective. *Consulting Psychology Journal: Practice and Research, 60*, 298-313.

Boyatzis, R. E., & Akrivou, K. (2006). The ideal self as a driver of intentional change. *Journal of Management Development, 25*, 624-642.

Bracken, D. W. & Rose, D. S. (2011). When does 360-degree feedback create behavior change? And how would we know it when it does? *Journal of Business and Psychology, 26*, 183-192.

Bracken, D. W., Rose, D. S., & Church, A. H. (in press). The evolution and devolution of 360° feedback. Industrial and Organizational Psychology: Perspectives on Science and Practice.

Brett, J. & Atwater, L. (2001). 360-degree feedback: Accuracy, reactions and perceptions of usefulness. *Journal of Applied Psychology, 86*, 930–942.

Brown, K. W. & Richard, M. (2003). The benefits of being present: Mindfulness and its role in psychological well-being. *Journal of Personality and Social Psychology, 84*, 822-848.

Caputo, P.M. & Roch, S. (2009, April). *Rating formats and perceptions of performance appraisal fairness.* Poster presented at the 24th meeting of the Society for Industrial and Organizational Psychology, New Orleans, LA.

Chen, Z., Williams, K., Fitness, J. & Newton, N. (2008). When hurt will not heal. Exploring the capacity to relive social and physical pain. *Psychological Perspectives, 19,* 789-795.

Cherniss, C. (2010). Emotional intelligence: Toward a clarification of a concept. *Industrial and Organizational Psychology Perspectives on Science and Practice, 3,* 110-126.

Conway, J. M., Lombardo, K., & Sanders, K. C. (2001). A meta-analysis of incremental validity and nomological networks for subordinate and peer ratings. *Human Performance, 14,* 267–303.

Cools, W., Hofmans, J., & Theuns, P. (2006). Context in category scales: Is "fully agree" equal to twice agree? European *Review of Applied Psychology, 56*, 223-229.

Conway, J. & Huffcutt, A. (1997). Psychometric properties of multi-source performance ratings: A meta-analysis of subordinate, supervisor, peer and self-ratings. Human *Performance, 10*, 331–360.

Chang, L. (1994). A Psychometric Evaluation of 4-Point and 6-Point Likert-Type Scales in Relation to Reliability and Validity. *Applied Psychological Measurement, 18*, 205-215.

Chemers, M. M., Watson, C. B. & May, S.T. (2000). Dispositional affect and leadership effectiveness: A comparison of self-esteem, optimism, and efficacy. *Personality and Social Psychology Bulletin, 26*, 267-277.

Chen, Z., Williams, K., Fitness, J. & Newton, N. (2008). When hurt will not heal. Exploring the capacity to relive social and physical pain. *Psychological Perspectives, 19*, 789-795.

Chiaburu, D. S., & Marinova, S. V. (2005). What predicts skill transfer? An exploratory study of goal orientation, training self-efficacy and organizational supports. *International Journal of Training and Development, 9*, 110–123.

Chiaburu, D. S., Van Dam, K., & Hutchins, H. M. (2010). Social support in the workplace and training transfer: A longitudinal analysis. *International Journal of Selection and Assessment, 18*, 187–200. doi: 10.1111/j.1468-2389.2010.00500.x

Cicchetti, D. V., Showalter, D., & Tyrer, P. J. (1985). The Effect of Number of Rating Scale Categories on Levels of Interrater Reliability: A Monte Carlo Investigation. *Applied Psychological Measurement, 9*, 31-36.

Conway, J. M., Lombardo, K., & Sanders, K. C. (2001). A meta-analysis of incremental validity and nomological networks for subordinate and peer ratings. *Human Performance, 14*, 267–303.

Conway, J. & Huffcutt A. (1997). Psychometric properties of multi-source performance ratings: A meta-analysis of subordinate, supervisor, peer and self-ratings. *Human Performance, 10*, 331-360.

Cools, W., Hofmans, J., & Theuns, P. (2006). Context in category scales: Is "fully agree" equal to twice agree? *European Review of Applied Psychology, 56*, 223-229.

Craig. S. B. & Hannum, K. (2006). Research update: 360-degree performance assessment. *Consulting Psychology Practice and Research, 58*, 117-122.

Dai, G., Stiles, P., Hallenbeck, G., & De Meuse, K. P. (2007, August). *Self-other agreement on leadership competency ratings: The moderating effects of rater perspectives and rating ambiguity.* Paper has been presented at the 2007 Annual Meeting of the Academy of Management, Philadelphia, PA.

Dawes, J. (2008). Do data characteristics change according to the number of scale points used? An experiment using 5-point, 7-point and 10-point scales. *International Journal of Market Research, 50,* *61-77.*

Dewall, C. N., MacDonald, G., Webster, G. D., Masten, C. L., Baumeister, R. F., Powell, C., Combs, D., Schurtz, D. R., Stillman, T. F., Tice, D. M. & Eisenberger, N. I. (2010). Acetaminophen reduces social pain: Behavioral and neural evidence. *Psychological Science, 21,* 931-937.

Dickerson, S. & Kemeny. M. (2004). Acute stressors and cortisol responses: A theoretical integration and synthesis of laboratory research. *Psychological Bulletin, 130,* 355-391.

Dunning, D., Heath, C. & Suls, J. (2004). Flawed self-assessment: Implications for health, education and the workplace. *Psychological Science in the Public Interest, 5,* 69-106.

Dweck, C.S. (1986). Motivational processes affecting learning. *American Psychologist, 41,* 1040-1048.

Dweck, C. & Leggett, E. (1988). A social-cognitive approach to motivation and personality. *Psychological Review, 95,* 256-273.

Eckert, R., Ekelund, B., Gentry, W. & Dawson, J. (2010). I don't see me like you see me but is that a problem? Cultural differences in rating discrepancy in 360-degree feedback instruments. *European Journal of Work and Organizational Psychology, 19,* 259-278.

Ehrlinger, J. (2008). Skill level, self-views and self-theories as sources of error in self-assessment. *Social and Personality Psychology Compass, 2,* 382-398.

Eisenberger, N. I., Lieberman, M. D. & Williams, K. D. (2003). Does rejection hurt? An fMRI study of social exclusion. *Science, 302,* 290–292.

English, A., Rose, D. & McClellan, J. (2009). *Rating Scale Label Effects on Leniency Bias in 360-degree Feedback.* Paper presented at the 24th Annual Meeting of the Society for Industrial Organizational Psychologist. New Orleans, LA.

Ericsson, K. (2006). *The influence of experience and deliberate practice on the development of superior expert performance.* In K.A. Ericsson et al., (Eds). *The Cambridge Handbook of Expertise and Expert Performance* (pp. 683-703). NY: Cambridge University.

Facteau, J. D. & Craig, S. B. (2001). Are performance appraisal ratings obtained from different rating sources comparable? *Journal of Applied Psychology, 86*, 215–227.

Fleenor, J., Taylor, S. & Chappelow, C. (2008). Leveraging the Impact of 360-degree Feedback. New York: John Wiley & Sons.

Fredrickson, B. L. (2013, July 15). Updated Thinking on Positivity Ratios. *American Psychologist*. Advance online publication. doi: 10.1037/a0033584

Fredrickson, B. L. & Losada, M. (2005). Positive affect and the complex dynamics of human flourishing. *American Psychologist, 60*, 678-686

Gentry, W. A. & Eckert, R. H. (2012). Integrating ILTs and fit into the development of global leaders: A 360-degree approach. *Industrial and Organizational Psychology: Perspectives on Science and Practice, 5*, 226-229.

Gentry, W. A., Yip, J., & Hannum, K. (2010). Self-observer rating discrepancies of managers in Asia: A study of derailment characteristics and behaviors in Southern Confucian Asia. *International Journal of Selection and Assessment, 18*, 237-250.

Gentry, W. A., Hannum, K. M., Ekelund, B. Z., & de Jong, A. (2007). A study of the discrepancy between self- and observer-ratings on managerial derailment characteristics of European managers. *European Journal of Work and Organizational Psychology, 16*, 295–325.

Goffin, R. D. & Anderson, D. W. (2002, June). *Differences in self and superior ratings of performance: Personality provides clues*. Paper presented at the Society for Industrial and Organizational Psychology, Toronto, Canada.

Goffin, R. & Anderson, D. (2007). The self-rater's personality and self-other disagreement in multi-source performance ratings: Is disagreement healthy? *Journal of Managerial Psychology, 22*, 271-

289.

Goffin, R. D. & Olson, J. M. (2011). Is it all relative? Comparative judgments and the possible improvement of self-ratings and ratings of others. *Perspective on Psychological Science, 6*, 48-60.

Goldsmith, M. (2009). How to spot the "uncoachables." Retrieved from http://blogs.hbr.org/goldsmith/2009/03/how_to_spot_the_uncoachables.html

Goldsmith, M. (2006). The Impact of Direct Report Feedback and Follow-Up on Leadership. Unpublished manuscript. www.marshallgoldsmith.com/articles

Gosling, S. D., John, O. P., Craik, K. & Robins, R. W. (1998). Do people know how they behave? Self-reported act frequencies compared with on-line codings by observers. Journal of Personality and Social Psychology, 74, 41–61.

Gollwitzer, P. M., & Sheeran, P. (2009). Self-regulation of consumer decision making and behavior: The role of implementation intentions. *Journal of Consumer Psychology, 19*, 593-607.

Gottman, J. M. (1994). *What predicts divorce? The relationship between marital processes and marital outcomes*. Hillsdale, NJ: Erlbaum.

Gregory, J. B., Levy, P. E. & Jeffers, M. (2008). Development of the feedback process within executive coaching. *Consulting Psychology Journal: Practice and Research, 60*, 42-56.

Greguras, G. J., & Robie, C. (1995). A new look at within-rater source inter-rater reliability of 360-degree feedback ratings. *Journal of Applied Psychology, 83*, 960–968.

Grossman, R., & Salas, E. (2011). The transfer of training: What really matters. *International Journal of Training and Development, 15*, 103–120.

Hannah, S. , Avolio, B. J. , Luthans, F. , & Harms, P. (2008). Leadership efficacy: Review and future directions. *Leadership Quarterly, 19*, 669-692.

Harris, M. & Schaubroeck, J. (1988). A meta-analysis of self-supervisor, self-peer, and peer-supervisor ratings. *Personnel Psychology, 41,* 43–62.

Harris, L. S. & Kuhnert, K. W. (2007). Looking through the lens of leadership: a constructive developmental approach. *Leadership & Organization Development Journal, 29,* 47-67.

Harris, M., & Schaubroeck, J. (1988). A meta-analysis of self-supervisor, self-peer and peer supervisor ratings. *Personnel Psychology, 41,* 43-62.

Heidemeier, H. & Moser, K. (2009). Self-other agreement in job performance ratings: A meta-analytics test of a process model. *Journal of Applied Psychology, 94,* 353-370.

Hirsh, J. B. & Inzlicht, H. (2008). The devil you know: Neuroticism predicts neural response to uncertainty. *Psychological Science, 19,* 962-967.

Hoffman, B., Lance, C. E., Bynum, B. & Gentry, W. (2010). Rater source effects are alive and well after all. *Personnel Journal, 63,* 119-151.

Hogan, J., Hogan, J. & Kaiser, R. (2011). Management derailment. APA handbook of industrial and organizational psychology, 3: Maintaining, expanding, and contracting the organization, APA Handbooks in Psychology (pp. 555-575).

Hogan, R. & Kaiser, R. (2005). What we know about leadership. *Review of General Psychology, 9,* 169-180.

Hölzel, B., Carmody, J., Vangel, M., Congleton, C., Yerramsetti, S., Gard, T. & Lazar, S.W. (2011). Mindfulness practice leads to increases in regional brain gray matter density. Psychiatry Research Neuroimaging, 191, 36-43.

Hoffman B. J. & Baldwin, S. P. (2012). Modern managerial assessment: A comparison of assessment centers and multisource feedback. In G. Thornton & N. Povah (Eds.), *Assessment centers and global talent management* (pp. 143-162). Burlington, VT: Gower.

Hoffman, B. J., Gorman, C. A., Blair, C. A., Meriac, J. P., Overstreet, B., & Atchley, E. K. (2012). Evidence for the effectiveness of an alternative multi-source performance rating methodology. *Personnel*

Psychology, 65, 531-563.

Hoffman, B. J., Lance, C. E., Bynum, B., & Gentry, W. (2010). Rater source effects are alive and well after all. *Personnel Journal, 63*, 119-151.

Hoffman B. J. & Woehr, D. J. (2009). Disentangling the meaning of multisource performance rating source and dimension factors. *Personnel Psychology, 62*, 735–765.

Hofstede, G. & McRae, R. R. (2004). Personality and culture revisited: Linking traits and dimensions of culture. *Cross-Cultural Research, 38*, 52-88. doi: 10.1177/1069397103259443

Hogan, R. (2007). *Personality and the fate of organizations.* Hillsdale, NJ: Erlbaum.

Hogan, R. & Kaiser, R. (2005). What we know about leadership. *Review of General Psychology, 9*, 169-180.

Holt, K. & Seki, K. (2012). Global leadership: A developmental shift for everyone. *Industrial and Organizational Psychology: Perspectives on Science and Practice, 5*, 198-217.

Hooijberg, R. & Lane, N. (2009). Using multisource feedback coaching effectively in executive education. *Academy of Management Learning and Education, 8,* 483-493.

Hyman, D. J., Pavlik, V. N., Taylor, W. C., Goodrich, G. K. & Moye, L. (2007). Simultaneous versus sequential counseling for multiple behavioral change. *Archives of Internal Medicine, 167,* 1152-1158.

Ilgen, D. & Davis, C. (2000). Bearing bad news: Reactions to negative performance feedback. *Applied Psychology: An International Review, 49*, 550-565.

Inceoglu, I. & Externbrink, K. (2012, April). *Leadership Development: Who knows best how well the Highflyers perform?* Paper presented at the 27th Annual Conference of the Society for Industrial and Organizational Psychology, San Diego, CA.

Jones, R. J., Woods, S. A., & Guilaume, Y. R. F. (20150). The effectiveness of workplace coaching: A meta-analysis of learning and performance outcomes from coaching. *Journal of Occupational and Organizational Psychology, 89*, 1-29.

Jordan, A. & Audia, P. (2012). Self-enhancement and learning from performance feedback. Academy of *Management Review, 37*, 211-231.

Joo, B. K. (2005). Executive coaching: A conceptual framework from an integrative review of research and practice. *Human Resource Development Review, 4*, 134-144.

Judge, T. A., Rodell, J. B.,Klinger, R. L., Simon, L. S., & Crawford, E. R. (2013). Hierarchical representations of the five factor model of personality in predicting job performance: Integrating three organizing frameworks with two theoretical perspectives. *Journal of Applied Psychology, 98*, 875-925.

Kaiser, R. & Overfield, D. (2011). Strengths, strengths overused, and lopsided leadership. *Consulting Psychology Journal: Practice and Research, 63*, 89-109.

Kaiser, R. B. & S. B. Craig. (2005). Building a better mouse trap: Item characteristics associated with rating discrepancies in 360-degree feedback. *Consulting Psychology Journal: Practice and Research, 57*, 235-245.

Kaplan, R. & Kaiser, R. (2009). Stop overdoing your strengths. Harvard Business Review, February 2009, 100-103.

Kaptchuk, T. J., Stason, W. B., Davis, R. B., Legedza, A. R., Schyer, R., Kerr, C. E., Stone, D. A, Nam, B. H., Kirsch, I. & Goldman, R. H. (2006). Sham device versus inert pill: a randomized controlled trial comparing two placebo treatments for arm pain due to repetitive strain injury. *British Medical Journal, 332*, 291-297.

Kilburg, R. (2006). Wisdom Mapping I: Self and Family Awareness. Executive Wisdom: Coaching and the emergence of virtuous leaders. *The Psychologist-Manager Journal, 10*, 145-167.

Klockner, K. & Hicks, R.E. (2008). My next employee: Understanding the Big Five and positive personality dispositions of those seeking psychological support interventions. *International Coaching*

Psychology Review, 3,148-163.

Kluger, A. & DeNisi (1996). The effects of feedback interventions on performance: A historical review, meta-analysis and preliminary feedback theory. *Psychological Bulletin, 119* , 254-285.

Koo, M. & Fishbach, A. (2010). Climbing the goal ladder: How upcoming actions increase level of aspiration. *Journal of Personality and Social Psychology, 99*, 1-13.

Kruger, J. & Dunning, D. (1999). Unskilled and unaware of it: How difficulties in recognizing one's own incompetence lead to inflated self-assessments. *Journal of Personality and Social Psychology, 77*, 1121-1134.

Lance, C. E., Hoffman, B. J., Gentry, W. & Baranik, L. E. (2008). Rater source factors represent important subcomponents of the criterion construct space, not rater bias. *Human Resources Management Review, 18*, 223-232.

Lozano, L. M., Garcia-Cueto, E. & Muniz, J. (2008). Effect of the number of response categories on the reliability and validity of rating scales. European Journal of *Research Methods for the Behavioral and Social Sciences, 4*, 73-79.

Luft, J. & Ingham, H. (1995). The Johari window, a graphic model of interpersonal awareness. Precedings of the western training Laboratory in group development. Los Angeles, UCLA.

Lally, P., Van Jaarsveld, C. Potts, H. & Wardle, J. (2009). How are habits formed: Modeling habit formation in the real world. *European Journal of Social Psychology, 1009*, 998-1009.

Law, K. S., Wong, C., & Song, L. J. (2004) The construct and criterion validity of emotional intelligence and its potential utility for management studies. *Journal of Applied Psychology, 89*, 483-496.

Lawton, R., Conner, M. & McEachan, R. (2009). Desire or reason: Predicting health behaviors from affective and cognitive attitudes. *Health Psychology, 28*, 56-65.

Le, H., Oh, I. S., Shaffer, J. A., & Schmidt, F. L. (2007). Implications of methodological advances for the practice of personnel selection:

How practitioners benefit from recent developments in meta-analysis. *Academy of Management Perspectives, 21*, 6–15.

Lebreton, J. M., Burgess, R. D., Kaiser, R. B., Atchley, E. K. & James, L. R. (2003). The Restriction of Variance Hypothesis and Interrater Reliability and Agreement: Are Ratings from Multiple Sources Really Dissimilar? *Organizational Research Methods, 6*, 80-12.

Lehman, B. J. & Conley, K. M. (2010). Momentary Reports of Social-Evaluative Threat Predict Ambulatory Blood Pressure. *Psychological Science and Personality Science, 1*, 51-56. doi: 10.1177/1948550609354924

Leonardelli, G. J., Herman, A. D., Lynch, M. E., & Arkin, R. M. (2003). The shape of self-evaluation: Implicit theories of intelligence and judgments of intellectual ability. *Journal of Research in Personality, 37*, 141–168.

Liao, S. C., Hunt, E. A., & Chen, W. Comparison between inter-rater reliability and inter-rater agreement in performance assessment. *Annals of the Academy of Medicine, Singapore. 39*, 613-618.

Libretto, J. M., Burgess, J. R. D., Kaiser, R. B., Archly, E. K., & James, L. R. (2003). The restriction of variance hypothesis and interpreter reliability and agreement: Are ratings from multiple sources really dissimilar? *Organizational Research Methods, 6,* 80–128.

London, M. & Smither, J. W. (2002). Feedback orientation, feedback culture and the longitudinal performance management process. *Human Resource Management Review, 12,* 81-100.

Losada, M., & Heaphy, E. (2004). The role of positivity and connectivity in the performance of business teams: A nonlinear dynamics model. *American Behavioral Scientist, 47,* 740–765.

Lozano, L. M., Garcia-Cueto, E., Muniz, J. (2008). Effect of the number of response categories on the reliability and validity of rating scales. *European Journal of Research Methods for the Behavioral and Social Sciences, 4,* 73-79.

Martin, H. J. (2010). Workplace climate and peer support as determinants of training transfer. *Human Resource Development Quarterly, 21*,

87–104.

Mashihi, S. & Nowack, K. (2013). *Clueless: Coaching people who just don't get it*. Santa Monica, CA: Envisia Learning, Inc.

McClelland, D. C. (1961). *The Achieving Society*. NY: Van Nostrand.

Morgeson, F. P., Mumford, T. V. & Campion, M. A. (2005). Coming full circle: Using research and practice to address 27 questions about 360-degree feedback programs. *Consulting Psychology Journal: Practice and Research, 57*, 3, 196-209.

Mund, M. & Mitte, K. (2011). The costs of repression: A meta-analysis on the relation between repressive coping and somatic diseases. *Health Psychology*, Advance online publication. doi: 10.1037/a0026257

Murphy, K. R. (2008). Explaining the weak relationship between job performance and ratings of job performance. *Industrial and Organizational Psychology, 1*, 148-160.

Murphy, K. R., Cleveland, J. N., & Mohler, C. (2001). *Reliability, validity and meaningfulness of multisource ratings*. In D. Bracken, C. Timmreck, and A. Church (Eds.), Handbook of multisource feedback (pp. 130–148). San Francisco: Jossey-Bass.

Ng, K. Y., Koh, C., Kennedy, J. & Chan, K. Y. (2011). Rating leniency and halo in multisource feedback ratings: Testing cultural assumptions of power distance and individualism-collectivism. *Journal of Applied Psychology, 96*, 1033-1044

Nieman-Gonder, J. (2006). *The effect of rater selection on rating accuracy*. Poster presented at the 21st Annual Conference of the Society for Industrial and Organizational Psychology, May 2006, Dallas, TX.

Nowack, K. (1992). Self-assessment and rater assessment as a dimension of management development. Human Resources Development Quarterly, 3, 141–155.

Nowack, K. (1993). 360 Degree feedback: The whole story. *Training & Development Journal, 47*, 69-72.

Nowack, K. (1997). Congruence Between Self and Other Ratings and Assessment Center Performance. *Journal of Social Behavior and Personality, 12*, 145-166.

Nowack, K. (1999a). *360-Degree feedback.* Intervention: 50 Performance Technology Tools San Francisco, Jossey-Bass, Inc., 34-46.

Nowack, K., Hartley, J. & Bradley, W. (1999b). Evaluating results of your 360-degree feedback intervention. *Training and Development, 53*, 48-53 Nowack, K. (2000). *Occupational stress management: Effective or not?* In P. Schnall, K. Belkie, P. Landensbergis, & D. Baker (Eds.), Occupational Medicine: State of the Art Reviews, (pp. 231-233). Hanley and Belfus, Inc., Philadelphia, PA.

Nowack, K. (2002). Does 360 Degree Feedback Negatively Affect Performance: Feedback Varies With Your Point of View. *HR Magazine, 47*,6.

Nowack, K. (2003). Executive Coaching: Fad or Future? *California Psychologist, 36*, 16-17.

Nowack, K. (2005). *Longitudinal evaluation of a 360 degree feedback program: Implications for best practices.* Paper presented at the 20th Annual Conference of the Society for Industrial and Organizational Psychology, Los Angeles, March 2005.

Nowack, K. (2006). Optimising Employee Resilience: Coaching to Help Individuals Modify Lifestyle. Stress News, *International Journal of Stress Management, 18*, 9-12.

Nowack, K. (2006). Emotional intelligence: Leaders Make a Difference. *HR Trends, 17*, 40-42.

Nowack, K. (2007). Why 360-Degree Feedback Doesn't Work. *Talent Management, 3*, 12.

Nowack, K. (2008). *Coaching for Stress: StressScan.* Editor: Jonathan Passmore, Psychometrics. In Coaching (pp. 254-274). Association for Coaching, UK.

Nowack, K. (2009). Leveraging Multirater Feedback to Facilitate Successful Behavioral Change. *Consulting Psychology Journal: Practice and Research, 61*, 280-297.

Nowack, K. (2011). Momentor Case Study: Leveraging the Impact of 360 Feedback. Unpublished Manuscript, Santa Monica, Envisia Learning. Inc.

Nowack, K. (2012). Emotional Intelligence: Defining and Understanding the Fad. *Training and Development*, 66, 60-63.

Nowack, K. & Mashihi, S. (2012). Evidence Based Answers to 15 Questions about Leveraging 360-Degree Feedback. *Consulting Psychology Journal: Practice and Research, 64*, 3, 157–182.

Nowack, K. M. (2015a). The Limits of Deliberate Practice. Talent Management Magazine, 11, 22-25.

Nowack, K. M. (2015b). Urban Talent Myths Exposed. Talent Management Magazine, 11, 35-37, 47.

Nowack, K. (2014). Taking the Sting Out of Feedback. Talent Development Magazine, 68, 50-54.

Oh, I. & Berry, C. M. (2009). The five-factor model of personality and managerial performance: Validity gains through the use of 360 degree performance ratings. *Journal of Applied Psychology, 94*, 1498-1513.

Olivero, G., Bane, D. & Kopelman, R. (1997). Executive coaching as a transfer of training tool: Effects on productivity in a public agency. *Public Personnel Management, 26,* 461–469.

Ones, D.S., Viswesvaran, C., & Schmidt, F.L. (2008) No new terrain: Reliability and construct validity of job performance ratings. *Industrial and Organizational Psychology, 1*, 174-179.

Ostroff, C., Atwater, L., & Feinberg, B. (2004). Understanding self-other agreement: A look at rater and ratee characteristics, context and outcomes. *Personnel Psychology 57*, 333-375.

Palmer, S. (2003). Health coaching to facilitate the promotion of healthy behaviour and achievement of health-related goals. *International Journal of Health Promotion & Education , 41* , 91-93.

Penny, J. (2003). Exploring differential item functioning in a 360-degree assessment: Rater source and method of delivery. *Organizational Research Methods, 6*, 61-79.

Pfau, B. & Kay, I. (2002). Does 360-degree feedback negatively affect company performance? *HR Magazine, 47*, 55-59.

Porr, D. & Fields, D. (2006). Implicit leadership effects on multi-source ratings for management development. *Journal of Managerial Psychology, 21*, 651–668.

Preston, C.C. & Colman, A.M. (2000). Optimal number of response categories in rating scales: Reliability, validity, discriminating power, and respondent preferences. *Acta Psychologica, 104*, 1-15.

Prochaska, J. O. & Velicer, W. F. (1997) The transtheoretical model of health behaviour change. American *Journal of Health Promotion, 12*, 38-48.

Quast, L. N. , Wohkittel, J. M., Chung, C., & Center, B. A. (2011, December). *Patterns of self-other rating discrepancies and predictions of managerial career derailment: Comparing Asia to the United States*. Paper presented at the 10th International Conference of the Academy of HRD (Asia Chapter) International Research Conference, Kuala Lumpur, Malaysia.

Quast, L. N., Center, B. A., Chung, C., Wohkittel, J. M., & Vue, B. (2011, February). *Using multi-rater feedback to predict managerial career derailment: A model of self-boss rating patterns*. Paper presented at the 2011 Academy of Human Resource Development International Research Conference in the Americas, Chicago, IL.

Rehbine, N. (2007). The impact of 360-degree feedback on leadership development. Unpublished doctoral dissertation, Capella University.

Reilly, R. R., Smither, J. W. & Vasilopoulos, N. L. (1996). A longitudinal study of upward feedback. *Personnel Psychology, 49*, 599-612.

Rock, D. (2008). SCARF: A brain based model for collaborating with and influencing others. *Neuroleaderhip Journal, 1*, 1-9.

Robie, S., Kaster, K., Nilsen, D. & Hazucha, J. (2000). The right stuff: Understanding cultural differences in leadership Performance. Unpublished Manuscript, Personnel Decisions, Inc.

Rhodes, R. E., Plotnikoff, R. C., & Courneya, K. S. (2008). Predicting the physical activity intention-behavior of adopters and maintainers using three social cognition models. *Annals of Behavioral Medicine, 36*, 244-252.

Roch, S. G., Sternburgh, A. M., & Caputo, P. M. (2007). Absolute vs. relative performance rating formats: Implications for fairness and organizational justice. *International Journal of Selection and Assessment, 15*, 302-316.

Rutledge, T. (2006). Defensive personality effects on cardiovascular health: A review of the evidence. In D. Johns (Ed), *Stress and its impact on society* (pp. 1–21). Hauppauge, NY: Nova Science Publishers.

Sala, F., & Dwight, S. (2002). Predicting executive performance with multi-rater surveys: Whom you ask makes a difference. *Journal of Consulting Psychology: Research and Practice, 54*, 166-172.

Schwartz, R. M., Reynolds, C. F., III., Thase, M. E., Frank, E., Fasiczka, A. L., & Haaga, D. A. F. (2002). Optimal and normal affect balance in psychotherapy of major depression: Evaluation of the balanced states of mind model. *Behavioural and Cognitive Psychotherapy, 30*, 439–450.

Scullen, S. E., Mount, M. K., & Goff, M. (2000). Understanding the latent structure of job performance ratings. *Journal of Applied Psychology, 85*, 956-970.

Sedikides, C. & Gregg, A. (2003). Self-enhancement: Food for thought. Perspectives on Psychological Science, 3, 102–116.

Sherman, S., & Freas, A. (2004). The Wild West of executive coaching. *Harvard Business Review, 82*, 82-90.

Shipper, F., Hoffman, R. & Rotondo, D. (2007). Does the 360 feedback process create actionable knowledge equally across cultures? *Academy of Management Learning & Education, 6*, 33-50.

Siefert, C., Yukl, G. & McDonald, R. (2003). Effects of multisource feedback and a feedback facilitator on the influence of behavior of managers toward subordinates. *Journal of Applied Behavior, 88*,

561-569.

Smith, P., Mustard, F. & Bondy, S. (2007). Examining the relationship between job control and health status: A path analysis approach. *Journal of Epidemiology &Community Health, 62*, 54-61.

Smither, J., London, M., & Reilly, R. (2005). Does performance improve following multisource feedback? A theoretical model, meta-analysis, and review of empirical findings. *Personnel Psychology, 58*, 33–66.

Smither, J., London, M., Flautt, R., Vargas, Y., & Kucine, I. (2003). Can working with an executive coach improve multisource feedback ratings over time? A quasi-experimental field study. *Personnel Psychology, 56*, 23–44.

Smither, J. & Walker, A.G. (2004). Are the characteristics of narrative comments related to improvement in 360-degree feedback ratings over time? *Journal of Applied Psychology, 89*, 575-581.

Smither, J. Walker, A. & Yap, M. (2004). An examination of web based versus paper and pencil upward feedback ratings. *Educational and Psychological Measurement, 64*, 40-61.

Smither, J., Brett, J., & Atwater, L. (2008). What do leaders recall about multi- source feedback? *Journal of Leadership and Organization Studies, 14*, 202-218.

Smither, J., London, M. & Richmond, K. (2005). The relationship between leaders' personality and their reactions to and use of multisource feedback: A longitudinal study. *Group & Organizational Behaviors, 30*, 181-210.

Taylor, S. E. & Brown, J. D. (1988). Illusion and well-being: A social psychological perspective on mental health. Psychological Bulletin, 103, 193–210.

Taylor, P., Taylor, H. & Russ-Eft, D. Transfer of management training from alternate perspectives. *Journal of Applied Psychology, 94*, 104-121.

Taylor, P., Taylor, H. & Russ-Eft, D. (2009). Transfer of management training from alternate perspectives. *Journal of Applied Psychology, 94,* 104-121.

Thach, E. (2002). The impact of executive coaching and 360-feedback on leadership effectiveness. *Leadership and Organization Development Journal, 23*, 205–214.

Wimer, S. & Nowack, K. (1998). Thirteen common mistakes in implementing multirater feedback systems. *Training and Development, 52,* 69-80.

Varela, O. E. & Premeaux, S. F. (2008). Do cross-cultural values affect multisource feedback dynamics? The case of high power distance and collectivism in two Latin American countries. *International Journal of Selection and Assessment, 16*, 134-142.

Viswanathan, M., Bergen, M., Dutta, S. & Childres, T. (1996). Does a single response category in a scale completely capture a response? *Psychology & Marketing, 13*, 457-479.

Vecchio, R. P. & Anderson, R. J. (2009). Agreement in self–other ratings of leader effectiveness: The role of demographics and personality. *International Journal of Selection and Assessment, 17*, 165-179.

Viswesvaran, C., Schmidt, F. L., & Ones, D. S. (2002). The moderating influence of job performance dimensions on convergence of supervisory and peer ratings of job performance: Unconfounding construct-level convergence and rating difficulty. *Journal of Applied Psychology, 87,* 345-354.

Viswesvaran, C., Schmidt, F. L., & Ones, D. S. (2005). Is there a general factor in ratings of job performance? A meta-analytic framework for disentangling substantive and error influences. *Journal of Applied Psychology, 90*, 108–131.

Wagner, R. & Goffin, R. (1997). Differences in Accuracy of Absolute and Comparative Performance Appraisal Methods. *Organizational Behavior and Human Decision Processes, 70*, 95-103.

Weng, L. (2004). Impact of the number of response categories and anchor labels on coefficient alpha and test-retest reliability. *Educational and Psychological Measurement, 64*, 956-972.

Wanguri, D. M. (1995). A review, an integration, and a critique of cross-disciplinary research on performance appraisals, evaluations, and feedback: 1980-1990. *The Journal of Business Communication, 32,* 267-293.

Weng, L. (2004). Impact of the number of response categories and anchor labels on coefficient alpha and test-retest reliability. *Educational and Psychological Measurement, 64,* 956-972.

Wikman, A. & Warneryd , B. (1990). Measurement errors in survey questions: Explaining response variability. *Social Indicators Research, 2,* 199–212.

Wilson, A. E. & Ross, M. (2001). From chump to champ: People's appraisals of their earlier and present selves. *Journal of Personality and Social Psychology, 80,* 572-584.

Woehr, D. J. (2008). On the relationship between job performance ratings and ratings of job performance: What do we really know? *Industrial and Organizational Psychology: Perspectives on Science and Practice, 1,* 161–166.

Woehr, D. J., Sheehan, M. K. & Bennett, W., Jr. (2005). Assessing measurement equivalence across rating sources: A multitrait–multi-rater approach. Journal of Applied Psychology, 90, 592–600.

Woo, S., Sims, C., Rupp, D. & Gibbons, A. (2008). Development engagement within and following developmental assessment centers: Considering feedback favorability and self-assessor agreement. *Personnel Psychology, 61,* 727-759.

Yukl, G., Gordon, A., & Taber, T. (2002). A hierarchical taxonomy of leadership behavior: Integrating a half century of behavior research. *Journal of Leadership and Organizational Studies, 9,* 15-32.

Zeidan, F., Johnson, S. K., Diamond, B. J., David, Z. & Goolkasian, P. (2010). Mindfulness meditation improves cognition: Evidence of brief mental training. *Consciousness and Cognition, 2,* 597-605.

PART III:
Encourage

Change before you have to.

JACK WELCH

Introduction:
Now That I Know Who I Am—Am I *Really* Ready For Change?

Eighty percent of success is showing up.

WOODY ALLEN

In the previous *Enlighten* section, we introduced a variety of exercises and techniques individuals can use to become more aware of their interpersonal style, personality, interests, values, social support, signature strengths, and potential development areas. As we have discussed, self-insight/self-awareness is a *necessary, but not sufficient, condition* for behavioral change. Too many times, we have been given feedback by others only to view it as incorrect, biased, judgmental, unfair, or simply inaccurate. In these cases we tend to react defensively and have little or no motivation to want to modify our own behaviors. Unless there is willingness and motivation to translate awareness into the deliberate practice of new behaviors, feedback only helps us to become more enlightened if we truly understand and accept the information shared with us. For example, we may learn that our blood pressure is dangerously high, but modifying our diet and exercising may not be something we are really committed to practice on a daily basis.

This *Encourage* section is about the process by which employees' motivation to change behavior is assessed and influenced to enable greater *readiness* to modify existing habits and patterns. During this stage, the coach determines whether the employee is ready to move forward and the amount of effort he or she is willing to exert. In addition to assessing motivation, determining a employee's readiness to change should also include a consideration of any personality factors that could potentially derail the behavioral change process.

The coach also encourages motivation by helping the employee envision the benefits of successful behavioral change, sometimes called a "What's-In-It-For-Me" (WIFM) approach by using a coaching technique called *Motivational Interviewing (MI)*. Motivational Interviewing is a structured approach that consultants can use to enhance employee motivation and commitment to action. MI describes techniques for discussing the differences between the personal outcomes that can be achieved by the employee's current behaviors and those that can be achieved by his or her ideal behaviors. In that sense, it is a means of exploring the WIFMs, as well as exploring the obstacles to achieving the employee's goals. One of the advantages to MI is that it is a collaborative, non-directive approach and is therefore more likely to lead to sustained behavioral change efforts (Passmore, 2007).

Another technique used in the *Encourage* stage is to utilize an individual *change model or theory* to help the employee better understand the typical stages that individuals progress through in a behavioral change effort. Once the coach and employee have chosen an appropriate method, they can provide a structured process for reviewing the feedback, ask reflective questions that increase motivation, and identify one or more competencies or specific actions to further develop. In order to accomplish this, consultants must be able to connect with their employees in a manner that motivates and inspires behavioral change. One simple approach to establishing this rapport is to tell relevant stories and link them back to an individual behavioral change model. For example in my own coaching practice, employees are particularly motivated when they can relate to someone who has successfully overcome similar work and life challenges and obstacles.

Once consultants have assessed readiness and motivation levels, they can help the employee identify next steps in the development journey (i.e., translating goal intentions to actual implementation). At this point, consultants and employees must reach an agreement in order to proceed with goal implementation stage. If the employee is not ready to change behavior, coaching might not be totally effective or even appropriate, unless the terminal goals are entirely to enhance insight and self-awareness. With unmotivated employees, consultants have to ask some important questions before they move ahead with the behavioral change intervention, such as:

- Does the employee possess an adequate environmental support system?
- Would another coach be more effective to motivate the employee?
- Is the employee's personality contributing to resistance, defensiveness, a lack of confidence to change, or an inability to handle ambiguity and challenges along the way?
- Does the employee have a record of prior failure in the behavioral goal they are tackling that might lead to diminished self-esteem and self-efficacy (e.g., weight loss)?

Whatever the reason, it may be necessary to come to terms with the situation *before* attempting to proceed with a potentially frustrating and futile process of behavioral change coaching. So, let's take a look at ways to assess the motivation to change in our employees and then how to move them along a readiness continuum to the actual implementation of specific and measurable development goals.

Factoid: New Year's Resolutions by the Numbers

1. Nearly four out of 10 adults will make one or more resolutions for the New Year, according to a study done by the University of Scranton.

2. After the first week of carrying out the goal, about 75 percent of people maintain their goal.

3. After week two, nearly 70 percent of people will maintain their goal.

4. After one month, about 64 percent will stick with their resolution.

5. After six months, about 46 percent of people are still on track with their goal.

Norcross, Mrykalo & Blagys, (2002)

Chapter 6:
Assessing Readiness to Change Behavior

> If you do not change direction, you may wind up where you are heading.
>
> ## LAO TZU

People only change behavior when they are sufficiently *motivated* to do so. The challenge, of course, is how to help employees who aren't motivated in the first place to increase their level of *readiness* to change and for those who are somewhat motivated to enhance their commitment to specific goals and actions.

One useful model that focuses specifically on the continuum of individual motivation to change behavior is called the Transtheoretical model of behavioral change (TTM). It offers some insight and suggestions for consultants about how to move employee's from a state of being completely unmotivated to a commitment of action as well as a employee's decision making processes.

Transtheoretical Model of Readiness to Change

In order to assess whether employees are ready to change, consultants may *first* need to understand the process by which change occurs. Prochaska & DiClemente's Transtheoretical Model (1983) has become a classic way of conceptualizing how individuals initiate change. It takes into account that most individuals do not change in a linear fashion but rather in a spiral in which relapse is fairly common for most complicated behavioral change efforts. The Transtheoretical Model outlines behavioral change as a process involving progress through a series of five "readiness" stages described below:

1. *Precontemplation* is the stage in which people are not intending to take action in the foreseeable future, usually measured as the next six months. People may be in this stage because they are uninformed or under-informed about the consequences of their behavior, or they may have tried to change a number of times and become demoralized about their ability to change. Both groups tend to avoid reading, talking, or thinking about their high-risk behaviors. They are often characterized in other theories as resistant or unmotivated, or as not ready for health promotion programs. The fact is, traditional health promotion programs are often not designed for such individuals and are not matched to their needs.

2. *Contemplation* is the stage in which people are intending to make some behavioral change efforts in the next six months. They are more aware of the pros of change but are also acutely aware of the cons. This balance between the costs and benefits of change can produce profound ambivalence that can keep people stuck in this stage for long periods of time (chronic contemplation or behavioral procrastination). These people are also not ready for traditional, action-oriented programs.

3. *Preparation* is the stage in which people are intending to take action in the immediate future, usually measured as the next month. They have typically taken some significant action in the past year. These individuals have developed a plan of action, such as joining a health education class, consulting a counselor, talking to a physician, buying a self-help book, or relying on a self-change approach. For example, these are the people that should be easily recruited for action-oriented leadership development, executive coaching, weight loss, or exercise programs.

4. *Action* is the stage in which people have made specific, overt modifications in their lifestyle practices within the past six months. Since action is observable, behavioral change often has been equated with action. But in the Transtheoretical Model, action is only one of five stages. The *action* stage is also the stage where vigilance against relapse is critical.

5. *Maintenance* is the stage in which people are working to prevent relapse, but they do not apply change processes as frequently as do people in action. They are less tempted to relapse and increasingly more confident that they can continue their change efforts over a specific period of time.

6. *Relapse* is often discussed as a distinct stage characterized by lapses and often full-blown relapses back to old behaviors. Some individuals rely primarily on change processes that have to do with contemplation and self-revaluation while they move into the action stage. They try to modify their behaviors by becoming more aware and gaining insight. Other individuals rely primarily on change processes that enable them to take action, without insight and awareness. These individuals may seem ready to change because they are taking action; however their lack of awareness may be likely to lead to temporary change (Prochaska, DiClemente, & Norcross, 1992). Awareness is one of the key elements that are vital for successful behavioral change (Nowack & Heller, 2001). Employees must know what it is about their behavior that is hindering their maximum potential before they can take action.

HR practitioners can use model to set expectations and facilitate the employee through the change process. In particular, the TTM *Preparation* stage of this model overlaps with our *Encourage* stage, where the employee prepares for goal setting and action.

Decisional Balance Force Field Analysis

One technique consultants can use to evaluate and modify change readiness is using the decisional balance Force Field analysis developed by Kurt Lewin. It states that change results from competition between *driving* and *restraining* forces (Dorn, 2008). It identifies forces that help reach the desired outcome and those that hinder that process. Driving forces can be thought of as problems or opportunities that provide motivation for change within the organization. Restraining forces are the various barriers to change.

Figure 3-1

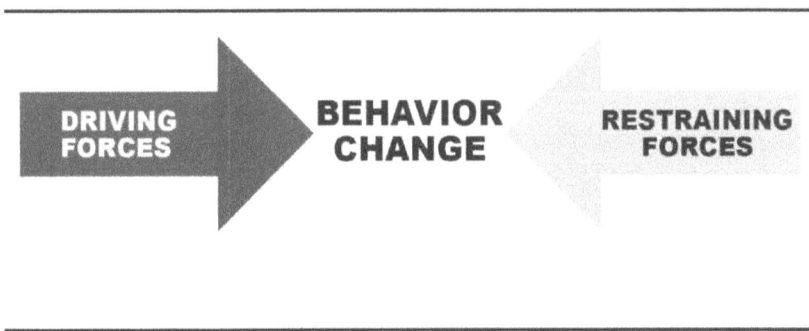

Driving Forces

Supporting forces will encourage your employee to succeed in your identified area of behavioral change. They tend to help initiate change and keep momentum over time. Support could come from your employee's manager and/or peers but it could also be their internal motivation to succeed in a new endeavor.

Restraining Forces

When considering the Force Field Analysis, Newton's third law of motion comes to mind: *"To every action, there is an equal and opposite reaction.*" For each supporting force, there is likely to be an opposite force that serves to impede behavioral change. These preventing forces could come from your employee's work environment or could be internal to their cognitive self-talk or attributional style. Force Field analysis focuses on ways of reducing the hindering forces and encouraging the positive ones. Force Field Analysis encourages agreement and reflection, through discussion of the underlying causes of a problem.

The decisional balance Force Field Analysis can help consultants weigh employee resistances against motivations of achieving change. The table below can help guide consultants in a step-by-step procedure of facilitating the decisional balance Force Field Analysis.

Figure 6-2

Force Field Analysis

Envisia Learning Change Model	Force Field Analysis Step	Facilitative Questions
ENLIGHTEN	**Step 1:** Defining the Problem	What is the nature of the current situation that is unacceptable and needs changing? It is useful to separate the specific problem from those things that aren't working well.
	Step 2: Defining the Change Objective	What is the desired situation that would be worth working toward? Be as specific as possible.
ENCOURAGE	**Step 3:** Identifying the Driving Forces	What are the factors that support change in the desired direction? What are the relative strengths of these forces? What are the inter-relationships between these driving forces?
	Step 4: Identifying the Restraining Forces	What are the factors that resist the proposed change and maintain the status quo? What are the inter-relationships between these restraining forces?
ENABLE	**Step 5:** Developing a Comprehensive Change Strategy	What can you do to strengthen and reinforce the "driving forces?" What can you do to remove or reduce any of the "restraining forces?"

Chapter 7:
Facilitating Motivation to Change Behavior

> It is not the strongest of the species that survives, not the most intelligent, but the one most responsive to change.

CHARLES DARWIN

As HR practitioners, we all come across our employees' resistance and ambivalence toward progress. We often hear clear indicators of a lack of motivation to change. Do any of these statements sound familiar from conversations you have had with your coaching employees?

- *"Unless I am able to achieve my goal quickly and with little effort, it isn't worth pursuing."*
- *"I don't become motivated through threats and a fear of punishment!"*
- *"The professionals who preach change don't know what they are talking about."*
- *"My problem behavior is not a big deal; I am in control at all times. Why all the fuss?"*
- *"Change should be simple and easy to achieve; why am I having so much trouble?"*
- *"The people around me constantly encourage me to change. It seems like I mean nothing to them unless I change."*
- *"The effort it takes to sustain change is too much; therefore, I will only work on attaining the change and leave sustaining the change for time to take care of."*
- *"If someone makes fun of or criticizes my efforts, I'll get*

demoralized and just give up."

- *"For me to be successful, it is important for everyone to understand me and my need to change."*
- *"People should realize how hard it is for me to change; they should be more sympathetic."*
- *"My friend's health habits are worse than mine. He seems fine! No one is asking him to change."*
- *"Unless everyone supports me, I'll never succeed in changing."*
- *"Why are they making this so difficult? Are they using scare tactics to make me change?"*
- *"This 'change thing'' is beginning to look like a plot by my manager who doesn't really understand me."*
- *"I've tried be*fore and wasn't successful so why do you think I will succeed now?"

Motivational Interviewing (MI) can help determine whether these types of comments represent a hindrance to change. There are two phases in Motivational Interviewing. The first phase involves *exploring ambivalence,* which includes building intrinsic motivation and self-efficacy for change. The second phase involves *strengthening the commitment to change* (Passmore & Tinwell, 2007).

Often, employees will demonstrate ambivalence when they feel reluctant to change. They may want to change, but they aren't deeply and intrinsically motivated. The coach's role is to help the employee examine the "costs" and "benefits" of changing. This approach can lead the employee to determine whether he or she feels it's worth it to continue with the behavioral change process.

Many consultants refer to "ballroom dancing" as a metaphor for Motivational Interviewing. Ballroom dancing can only occur when two people move together in a partnership. When done well, the movement unfolds through a series of subtle presses, or influences. As consultants, we do want to influence our employees to change, but we don't want to manipulate them into making changes that they are not ready for. Thus, the prescription for change must match the employee's motivation level. A employee that is very motivated may be willing to do more than a employee that is moderately motivated (Passmore & Tinwell, 2007).

> ## Factoid: Rehab is for Quitters
>
> Psychologists Gregory Miller and Carsten Wrosch have found that when people quit unattainable goals, they may have better mental and physical health than those who persevere (Miller & Wrosch 2007). These findings build on previous research, which found that persistent individuals experienced higher levels of an inflammatory protein called C-reactive protein (an indicator of stress), as well as increased cortisol. They also reported lower psychological well-being.

Coaching Techniques for Effective Motivational Interviewing and Readiness Assessment

It is important for consultants to approach their employees in a non-judgmental manner, so those employees can appropriately identify their resistance. The following principles can help consultants increase a employee's awareness about his or her resistance to change and, similarly, his or her motivation to change (Miller & Rollnick, 2002).

- *Express empathy,* by using reflective listening to convey an understanding of the employee's point-of-view and underlying drives.
- *Develop the discrepancy* between the employee's most deeply held values and current behavior.
- *Manage resistance,* by responding with empathy and

understanding, rather than confrontation.

- *Support self-efficacy,* by building the employee's confidence that change is possible.

Motivational Interviewing Case Study

Throughout the next section, we will review each of these techniques and encourage your application of them by utilizing the case study below to identify and overcome a employee's ambivalence to change.

Chris is Senior Executive at a highly profitable manufacturing firm. He has a large team, and he seems to lack the interpersonal and leadership skills needed to fully engage and empower them based on his recent performance evaluation and 360-degree feedback results. Feedback from his manager and team indicate that he does not demonstrate a highly participative or involvement-oriented leadership style, does not solicit input from others, and does not involve his team in problem solving, decision making, or planning.

He is perceived to be highly defensive when constructive suggestions are given to him. In fact, when an external coach hired by the company met with Chris to review his 360-degree results with him, he demonstrated resistance toward changing any leadership practices and behaviors.

Motivational Interviewing Exercise #1:

Express Empathy Using OARS

Expressing empathy involves seeing the world through the employee's eyes, thinking about things like the employee thinks about them, feeling things like the employee feels them, and sharing in the employee's experiences. The expression of empathy is a critical element of Motivational Interviewing. When employees feel understood, they are better able to open up to their own motivations and resistance. The sharing of experiences allows consultants to assess when and where employees need support and what potential pitfalls employees can focus on. As a result, employees' defensiveness is disarmed, and they can actually accept their feelings of reluctance toward changing.

"OARS" is an acronym used to describe some of the *micro-skills* involved in expressing empathy with employees in a coaching intervention. "OARS" stands for *O*pen-ended questions, *A*ffirmations, *R*eflective listening, and *S*ummarizing. The most effective consultants tend to utilize the OARS technique as part of their coaching "toolbox" with their employees.

Directions: Practice applying each of the OARS micro-skills by writing a response you might have to Chris' statements below based on the case study presented earlier.

> <u>Chris:</u> *"I am completely surprised with my 360-degree feedback results. I have been one of the top performers in this department for many years so I can't really understand how nobody has shared any of these perceptions or issues with me before. I'm guessing that it's just a few critics that don't really reflect how the majority of my direct reports, peers and manager really view me."*

Open-ended Questions

Write an open-ended question in response to the statement that Chris made about his reaction to his 360-degree feedback results. Ensure you are asking questions in a way that allows Chris to open up.

Coach Response:

Affirmations
Write a response that ensures Chris feels valued and appreciated. Make sure you are providing positive reinforcement as you affirm Chris.
Coach Response:

Reflective Listening
Write a response that ensures Chris feels understood. Make sure you are seeking to clarify how Chris feels.
Coach Response:

Summarizing
Write a response that demonstrates that you have a clear understanding of Chris' situation. Summarize what you have understood in terms of the content of the conversation.
Coach Response:

Motivational Interviewing Exercise #2:

Identify Discrepancies

One important Motivational Interviewing skill is developing employees' awareness of the discrepancies between their current behaviors and ideal behaviors. By identifying and clarifying discrepancies, ambivalence and resistance are uncovered. Once employees see these discrepancies more clearly, they can begin to elicit change statements that enhance their motivation to want to initiate new behaviors.

Assessing discrepancies between employees' current states versus their future states can be illustrated through the use of *Motivational*

Rulers. This is a technique suggested by Miller and Rollnick (2002) that a coach can utilize to assess an employee's stage of change. For example, motivation to change can be assessed by simply asking the employee to rate the *perceived readiness to change* on a scale of 0 to 10, with 0 being "not at all interested in changing," and "10" meaning "they have already made the change." To assess *confidence to change*, a confidence "ruler" can be employed by the coach: "Why are you an X on the scale and not a zero?" "What would it take for you to go from X to a higher number?" Both of these "change rulers" help to elicit "change talk," which helps the employee begin to see the advantages of initiating new behaviors and building confidence that can be successful over time.

Direct ions: In the space below, pose a question to Chris, utilizing either the readiness or confidence ruler to elicit "change talk", and explore in what way Chris feels a sense of control and optimism to succeed in his behavioral change efforts.

Identifying Discrepancies Exercise

Coach Response:

Motivational Interviewing Exercise #3:

Roll with Resistance

The role of the coach is not to confront or argue with a employee's possible defensiveness or resistance to changing behavior but to "roll with it." Statements demonstrating resistance shouldn't be challenged! Instead, the coach can disarm this defensiveness by reflecting on the employee's statements in a neutral way that validates the employee's concerns. By using this approach, resistance decreases, as employees become less argumentative and less likely to play "devil's advocate" to the coach's suggestions. As a result, new perspectives are examined without imposing anything upon them.

Four techniques can be used to help employees move through resistance and increase their willingness to initiate or continue with successful change efforts. These include: 1) Reflection (seeking to understand your employee's perspective through paraphrasing content and reflecting feelings expressed); 2) Shifting Focus (helping the employee become solution focused through questions); 3) Agreement with a Twist (agreeing with your employee and attempting to point out something they may have not fully considered or thought about); and 4) Reframing (suggesting a benefit or positive outcome of the behavioral change effort). Each of these when used strategically can be highly effective to help your employee overcome potential barriers to implementing and sustaining new behaviors and practices.

Directions: Practice "rolling with resistance" by writing your responses to Chris' statements in the boxes below.

> <u>Chris:</u> *"If my staff demonstrated that they were competent, maybe I would be a bit more involvement oriented or participative and allow them to take the lead on decisions more frequently. Most are just too inexperienced or not motivated for me to trust they will come up with high quality decisions. I can't afford not to succeed at this stage of my career."*

Reflection

Write a response that allows Chris to reflect on his resistant statements. For example, listen and summarize Chris' resistant statements in a way that conveys understanding and empathy of Chris' feelings.

Coach Response:

Shifting Focus

Write a response that helps Chris shift thoughts from obstacles and barriers to possible solutions.

Coach Response:

Agreement with a Twist

Write a response that demonstrates your agreement, with a slight twist, that moves the discussion forward.

Coach Response:

Reframing

Write a statement to reframe Chris' view by focusing on potential benefits or positive outcomes of behavior change.

Coach Response:

Motivational Interviewing Exercise #4:

Support Self-Efficacy for Change Talk

As employees are held responsible for choosing and carry ing out actions necessary for change, consultants can help them focus on staying motivated by reinforcing and supporting their sense of self-efficacy and self-esteem. It's quite simple: If the employee truly believes he or she can and will change, then he or she will. For example, the coach might remind the employee about other successes he or she has made recently or explore his/her way of explaining previous successes.

Believe in the Employee's Ability to Change

Write a statement that demonstrates confidence in Chris' skills, abilities or desires to be successful with change effort.

Coach Response:

Directions: Demonstrate this technique by writing sentences that would support Chris' self-efficacy in the boxes below.

Identify Signature Strengths

Write a statement that probes to uncover "signature strengths" (a skill that Chris is both competent and passionate about).

Coach Response:

Exploring Employee Motivation through their Attributional Style

Attributional style is the approach that employees use to explain their success and failures. If you listen carefully to your employee, you will uncover three components:

1. **Internal versus External Perspective**. This involves how the employee explains where the cause of an event arises. People experiencing events may see themselves as the cause (internal) versus as a result of circumstances that are outside their influence (external).

2. **Permanent versus Temporary Perspective**. This involves how the employee explains the extent of the cause. Employees who see things as permanent typically see the situation as unchangeable and will continue indefinitely as opposed to

being short-term and over in some period of time.

3. **Pervasive or Specific Perspectiv**e. This involves how the employee explains the extent of the effects. Employees may see the situation as affecting all aspects of life (pervasive) or only this unique situation (specific).

Attributional style can be either described as optimistic or pessimistic. For example, employees who generally tend to blame themselves for negative events or failures in their life believe that such events are a direct result of their efforts, will continue indefinitely, and describe their lives in general. During the last 25 years, studies have shown that employees who profess pessimistic explanations for life events have poorer physical health, are more prone to depression, and have a less adequately functioning immune system (Peterson, 2000).

A pessimistic attributional style might interfere with successful goal setting and implementation. Consultants might consider using the exercises developed for this section with their employees to help assess their primary attributional style and help build a more optimistic explanation for the future to facilitate behavioral change success.

Sample OARS Exercise Answers

Open-ended Questions

Coach Response: *"What do you see as some of the positive advantages of being seen as more participative?"*

Coach Response: *"What's preventing you from getting started? Why?"*

Affirmations

Coach Response: *"You have demonstrated success in your work and performance. I believe your competence can help you achieve what you want to achieve."*

Coach Response: *"You have risen through the ranks at your firm. You have a consistent track record as a high performer also It appears that you must be able to work with different types of colleagues and team members if you want to."*

Reflective Listening

Coach Response: *"Chris, I get a sense that there is a lot on your plate right now, and that seems a bit overwhelming."*

Coach Response: *"You seem to be suggesting that acting closer to your team can actually hinder their performance on the job. Is that right?"*

Summarizing

Coach Response: *"Chris, what I'm getting from what you are saying is, ..."*

Coach Response: *"You seem to be saying....."*

Sample Motivational Interviewing Exercise Answers

Identify Resistance

Coach Response: *On a scale of 1 to 10, how confident are you that if you made a decision to change, that you could change, with 1 representing not at all confident and 10 representing extremely confident? What led you to choose a 7, rather than a 3?*

Coach Response: *What would it take to move you from a 7 to an 8? Why are you a 7 on the scale and not a zero? What would it take for you to go from 7 to a higher number?*

Reflection

Coach Response: *"You seem to be saying that your direct reports, colleagues, and managers are overreacting."*

Coach Response: *"You seem to see the value of being more participative but feel as if it is a perspective not viewed equally by everyone on your team."*

Shifting Focus

Coach Response: *"Can you think about some of the positive consequences of making the changes we have discussed today either for you or your team?"*

Coach Response: *"You have described some good reasons for the situation. What do you see as some possible solutions that you can influence directly?"*

Agreement with a Twist

Coach Response: *"You've made a good point, and that's important. You are absolutely correct to point out that some of your some of your direct reports that your inherited aren't truly motivated or competent. What things can you influence and/or control though to increase their level of commitment and engagement on the job?"*

Coach Response: *"I see your point of view. We know that high potential talent expect leaders to constructively confront poor performance on a team. Any thoughts on how you can keep your high potential talent engaged and committed to the organization?"*

Reframing

Coach Response: *"I understand that you want to have a productive, hard-working team, let's explore some possibilities of LEADING them to ensure that they stay on top of their work."*

Coach Response: *"Despite those challenges, I sense that you are determined and that this change is important to you."*

Sample Motivational Interviewing Exercise Answers

Identify Signature Strengths

Coach Response: *"Chris, you are recognized as a top producer. What are some of the skills and qualities that you think have contributed towards your success?"*

Coach Response: *"Chris, name a time in your life when you had to overcome a huge obstacle. What did you do? How did you do it? What skills allowed you to become successful?"*

Identify Areas for Improving Skills & Efficacy

Coach Response: *"Chris, if you were a coach and I was your employee, what would you advise me to do more, less or differently?"*

Coach Response: *"Chris, you have obviously demonstrated competence on many levels, according to your 360-degree feedback results. How can you utilize that competence to work on your perceived improvement a r e a s ?"*

Believe in the Employee's Ability to Change

Coach Response: *"Chris, I'm impressed with your ability to stay focused on your behavior change goals given everything on your plate—truly impressive so keep up the great work!"*

Coach Response: *"I'd like to have a dozen employees like you that demonstrate the drive and commitment to move ahead despite some realistic challenges and barriers you have faced."*

Reinforce Change Talk

Coach Response: *"Can you name one person that you admire who has succeeded in changing his/her habits? What did they do? Is change possible?"*

Coach Response: *"Suppose you were the coach and I had some of these perceived areas for development. Based on that, what would you tell me?"*

Figure 6-3

Seven Tips on Assessing Employee Motivation

1.	Seek to understand the employee's frame of reference.
2.	Reinforce employee's thoughts, so that statements encouraging change are amplified and statements that reflect the status quo are dampened down.
3.	Facilitate employee statements that encourage change, such as expressions of problem recognition, concern, desire, the intention to change, and the ability to change.
4.	Identify the employee's stage of change and use stage appropriate techniques to increase "readiness" to change.
5.	Express acceptance and affirmation.
6.	Affirm the employee's freedom of choice and self-direction.
7.	Allow the employee's resistance to exist. Don't argue with them!

Summary

People don't initiate new behaviors and sustain them over time *unless they are sufficiently motivated.* One of the important roles of coaching is to help employees increase their readiness to change behavior and translate goal intentions into actual implementation.

Motivational Interviewing (MI) is proven and structured approaches to help employees better understand their ambivalence about changing behaviors and increasing a desire to do things more, less, or differently to enhance their effectiveness. Using motivational interviewing techniques like the *Change Ruler* to facilitate "change talk" can help employees see the advantages of initiating and sustaining new behaviors. Another way to assess motivation is through identifying their attributional style in order to learn about employee perceptions of prior behavioral change success and failures that might be beneficial or impede future change attempts. Consultants should become familiar with one or more of the theories and models of individual behavioral change and apply some of their techniques and exercises to help foster motivation and a sense of confidence to succeed in behavioral change efforts.

Recent research suggests that attempts to change people's intentions alone may not always result in successful maintenance of behavior over time (Lawton, Cooner & McEachan, 2009). Many employees often express a strong desire and intent to become more effective and to try new behaviors, but oftentimes, they rarely initiate or sustain a new change for very long.

Some recent evidence suggests that *perceived importance and concern* for the desired behavioral change end-point might be the *best predictor* differentiating non-intenders from those who are successful adopters of new behavior, whereas self-efficacy, perceived control, and being clear about the "cons" behind behavioral change are more important in discriminating successful maintainers from unsuccessful maintainers (Rhodes, Plotnikoff & Courneya, 2009).

Key Points

1. Nobody likes a change, except for wet babies. Keep in mind that unless an employee understands and accepts feedback and is willing to use it to improve, his or her behavior will likely remain the same, despite anything a coach does.

2. Consultants need to help employees explore the advantages and disadvantages of changing behavior. Helping employees begin to talk about the advantages of change helps to convert *intentions* into actual *implementation* of goals.

3. Not all people who express an interest to change behavior will necessarily be *successful* in either implementing new behaviors or sustaining them over time. Behavioral change is complex, and consultants not only need to assess their employee's internal motivation and readiness stage but the external support and environment that can help reinforce or punish new behaviors.

4. Pessimistic attributional styles (explanations of life events as being internal, permanent, and invasive) are likely to undermine a employee's successful pursuit of behavioral change efforts and contribute to both psychological distress and helplessness.

Encourage References

Dolan, M. J., Seay, T. A. & Vellela, T. C. (2006). The Revised Stage of Change Model and the Treatment Planning Process. Compelling Perspectives on Counseling. *Journal of Counseling and Psychotherapy, 3*, 79-94.

Dorn, F.J. (2008, April). Change Management: Theory and practice, strategies and techniques. Paper presented at the American Psychological National Conference, Boston, MA.

Fishbein, M. & Ajzen, I. (1975). Belief, attitude, intention, and behavior: An introduction to theory and research. Reading, MA: Addison-Wesley.

Kotter, J. P. (1996). *Leading Change*. Boston: Harvard Business School Press.

Lawton, R., Conner, M. & McEachan, R. (2009). Desire or reason: Predicting health behaviors from affective and cognitive attitudes. *Health Psychology, 28*, 56-65.

McEvoy, P. & Nathan, P. (2007). Perceived costs and benefits of behavioral change: Reconsidering the value of ambivalence for psychotherapy outcomes. *Journal of Clinical Psychology, 63*, 1217-1229.

Miller, W. R. & Rollnick, S. (2002). Motivational Interviewing: *Preparing People for Change,* 2nd ed., New York: Guilford Press; 2002.

Miller, W. R. & Rollnick, S. (2009). Ten things that motivational interviewing is not. *Behavioural and Cognitive Psychotherapy, 200 9*, 37, 129-140.

Miller, G. E. & Wrosch, C. (2007). You've gotta know when to fold'em: Goal disengagement and systemic inflammation in adolescence. *Psychological Science, 18*, 773-777.

Norcross, J., Mrykalo, S. & Blagys, M. (2002). Auld Lang Syne: Success predictors, change processes, and self-reported outcomes of New

Year's resolvers and nonresolvers. *Journal of Clinical Psychology, 58*, 397-405.

Nowack, K. & Heller, B. (2001). Making executive coaching work: The importance of emotional intelligence. *Training Magazine*, trainingmag.com.

Passmore, J. (2007). Motivational interviewing – ambivalence, intrinsic motivation, and self-efficacy. Addressing deficit performance through coaching – using motivational interviewing for performance improvement at work. *International Coaching Psychology Review, 2,* 265-275.

Peterson, C. Optimistic explanatory style and health. In: J.F. Gilham (Ed.). The science of optimism and hope: Research essays in honor of Martin E.P. Seligman (pp. 145-162). Philadelphia: Templeton Foundation.

Prochaska, J. O., Diclemente, C. C. & Norcross, J. C. (1997). *In search of how people change: Applications to addictive behaviors.* In A. G. Marlatt and G. R. VandenBos (Eds), Addictive behaviors: Readings on etiology, prevention, and treatment (pp.671-696). Washington, DC, US: American Psychological Association.

Rhodes, R. E., Plotnikoff, R. C. & Courneya, K. S. (2008). Predicting the physical activity intention-behavior of adopters and maintainers using three social cognition models. *Annals of Behavioral Medicine, 36*, 244-252.

PART IV:
Enable

When it is obvious that the goals cannot be reached, don't adjust the goals; adjust the action steps.

CONFUCIUS

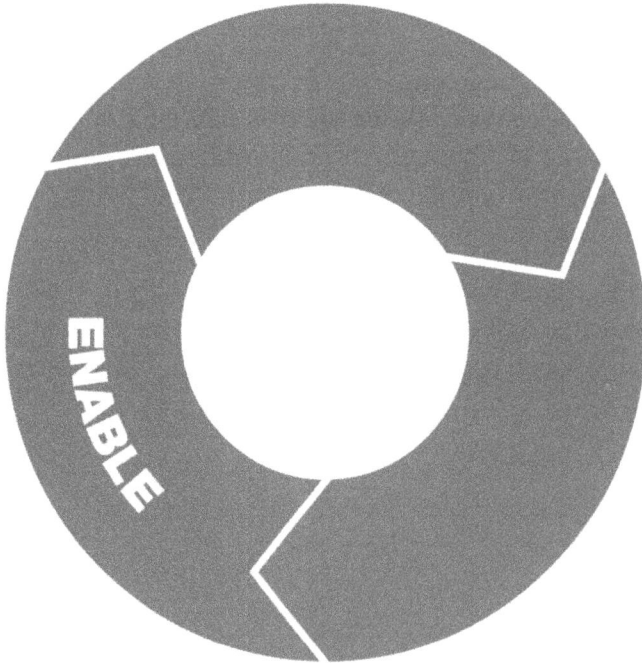

Introduction:
How Do I Go About Changing?

> You miss 100 percent of the shots you don't take.

WAYNE GRETZKY

If three squirrels are sitting on a tree and two decide to jump off to another branch, how many are left? The answer is three. You might ask why but the answer is simple because there is a big difference between *deciding* and actually *doing*. A strong intention to act does not guarantee behavioral change. This is the difference between *goal intentions* and *implementation intentions*. People often fail because they may confront problems during the process of attaining their goals; that is, they either fail to get started or they get derailed along the way.

Factoid: Intentions Are Overrated

A review of health behavior practices (e.g., condom use, exercise, cancer screening) found that people acted on their strong intentions only 53 percent of the time (Gollwitzer & Sheeran, 2006).

Not all enlightened and truly motivated employees are successful at changing their styles or specific behaviors that may contribute to future "derailment." This *Enable* section describes the process of setting and accomplishing goals. It begins by providing ways to design goals that will increase the likelihood of attaining them. It then details the process for and components of turning new behavioral practices into long-term habits. This section will then move on to describing ways relapse occurs and provides preventative intervention strategies. It ultimately identifies various methods and approaches for talent development and sustaining change, and it introduces the Envisia Learning, Inc. *Performance Coaching Model* to target internal and external coaching of talent at all levels of the organization.

Chapter 8:
Goal Setting

> The tragedy in life doesn't lie in not reaching your goal. The tragedy lies in having no goal to reach.
>
> **BENJAMIN MAYS**

Formulating goals is a *key* to successful implementation. People are much more likely to develop when they decide which competencies or skills to focus on. Goals should include clear actions that break down learning into manageable steps. For example, when a employee achieves success on specific developmental goals, it paves the way for setting new and more challenging goals. It is important to stretch individuals by structuring goals into small, attainable, and manageable steps. Generally, in order to stretch employees, it is particularly important to maximize choice.

Consultants have two primary roles to help their employees with the goal setting process: 1) Helping employee set development goals; and 2) Providing ongoing feedback regarding progress. Beck and his colleagues argue that in order for consultants to help their employees develop awareness, skills and abilities, they should take a "multiple goal perspective" (Beck, Gregrory & Carr, 2009). They emphasize three important recommendations to help employees pursue both developmental goals in tandem with regular work goals:

1. Set development goals with high expectancies. It is important that the goals set by employees are achievable and to set goals early on that are easily accomplished (research suggests that goals that can be achieved easily help build self-efficacy).

2. Provide feedback development progress. Beck et al. (2009) point out that goals that receive the most feedback are typically perceived to be most important and this translates into more time and effort on behalf of the employee. Such feedback should be given with careful attention to the learning style and personality of the employee.

3. Identify incentives for development. Consultants should help employees identify incentives that are associated with their development goals to enhance motivation and minimize relapse (e.g., emphasizing future outcomes and rewards).

Indeed, the coach typically plays a large role in the goal setting process. He or she may want to refrain from providing the goals to his or her employee. Rather, the employee should be able to generate his or her own goals, with the help of the coach to refine them. Some research has indicated that the employee's involvement in setting his or her own goals, either autonomously or collaboratively increases the commitment to the goals, when compared to goals that are instead assigned to them (Locke & Latham, 2002).

Factoid: What's More Motivating—Focusing on What Has Been Completed or What Is Left to Do?

A focus on remaining (vs. completed) actions increases the motivation to move up to a more advanced level, whereas the focus on completed (vs. remaining) actions increases the satisfaction derived from the present level (Koo & Fishback, 2010). Focusing on remaining (vs. completed) actions leads people to choose a more challenging level for their next goal.

Goal Setting Factors

In order to effectively establish goals, it is a good idea to consider all the factors involved. There are a number of variables that influence the level of goal pursuit individuals engage in (Koo & Fishbach, 2010). Some of these variables include the difficulty of attaining the goal or the designated timeframe for that attainment (Shilts, Horowitz, & Townsend, 2004). Other factors that determine the success or failure of attaining goals include personality factors and the personal habits of the employee. Let's look at five important factors that affect goal setting and successful accomplishment.

1. *Goal Difficulty*

    Research suggests that challenging goals lead to greater effort, focus, and persistence compared to difficult or easy goals. People who perceived their goal as difficult to attain reported higher positive emotion, increase in job satisfaction, and perceptions of occupational success (Latham & Locke, 2008).

2. *Proximity*

    Goals are often distinguished by how far forward they project into the future. Schunk (2001) suggests that proximal short-term goals are achieved more quickly and result in higher motivation and better self-regulation than more distant and long-term goals. Further, these researchers suggest that if long-term goals must be established, subdividing them can produce greater benefits.

3. *Time Frame*

    The time frame for completion needs to be reasonable in order for goals to be attained (Latham & Locke, 2006). Research suggests that individuals are more likely to maintain goals in the face of obstacles when more time remained for goal pursuit than when less time remained. (Schmidt & Deshon, 2007).

4. *Multiple Goals*

Individuals can accomplish more than one goal at a time, assuming that these goals do not conflict with each other in some way (Locke & Latham, 1990). It becomes difficult to achieve multiple goals when each goal alone is attainable, but together the goals cause conflict (Schunk, 2002).

5. *Specificity*

Research shows that *specific* goals raise performance because they clarify the amount of effort required for success. They also boost self-efficacy and confidence by providing a clear standard against which to determine progress (Schunk, 2002).

Goal Characteristics

In discussing goals, it is important to separate the goal setting from the goal striving process. Prior to goal striving, people need to choose specific goals, and several variables affect which goals they are more likely to set for themselves. For example, a person may choose goals associated with positive feelings, goals that fulfill basic needs (e.g., the need to belong), goals family members hold for the individual, and even contagious goals the person seeks from observing others.

Psychologists have studies a number of important characteristics of goals that are associated with success. There are a number of characteristics that directly influence the goal pursuit individuals engage in (Koo & Fishbach, 2010). Some of these characteristics include proximity of the end state (e.g., distant vs. far away), motivational mindset (e.g., avoidance vs. approach), difficulty (e.g., challenging vs. easy), type of goal (e.g., learning vs. performance), and number of goals to tackle at one time (e.g., single vs. multiple). Each of these is briefly described below.

1. *Easy vs. Challenging Goals*

Previous findings have traditionally emphasized that goals should not be overly ambitious as exemplified by the SMART goal acronym, which suggests that goals should be Specific, Measurable, Attainable, Realistic, and Timely (Latham, 2003). However, current research suggests that *challenging* goals lead to greater effort, focus, and persistence than moderately difficult or easy goals.

It has also been suggested that people who perceived their goal as difficult to attain reported higher positive emotion, an increase in job satisfaction, and perceptions of occupational success (Latham & Locke, 2008). In fact, there is some evidence that unrealistic goals might actually inspire, rather than, interfere with goal pursuit (Linde, Jeffrey, Finch, Ng, & Rothman, 2004).

2. *Distant vs. Far Away*

Goals are often distinguished by how far forward they project into the future. Schunk (2001) suggests that short-term goals are achieved more quickly, result in higher motivation, and better self-regulation than more distant and long-term goals. Further, these researchers suggest that if long-term goals must be established, subdividing or "chunking" them into more manageable tiny actions or steps can produce greater benefits. Additionally, the time frame for completion needs to be reasonable in order for goals to be attained (Latham & Locke, 2006). Research suggests that individuals are more likely to maintain goals in the face of obstacles and challenges when more time remained for goal pursuit than when less time remained. (Schmidt & Deshon, 2007).

3. *Single vs. Multiple Goals*

Behavior change efforts are often not linear but tend to be progressive, regressive or even static. Current findings suggest that multiple simultaneous efforts (e.g., behaviors planned to improve multiple competencies at the same time) tend to be equal or even more effective than focusing on single goals because they reinforce quick benefits (Hyman, Pavlik, Taylor, Goodrick, & Moye, 2007).

Individuals can accomplish more than one goal at a time, assuming that these goals do not conflict with each other in some way (Locke & Latham, 1990). It becomes difficult to achieve multiple goals when each goal alone is attainable, but together the goals cause conflict (Schunk, 2002).

4. *Learning Goals vs. Performance Goals*

An individual's goal orientation describes the goals that they choose and the methods used to pursue those goals (DeShon & Gillespie, 2005). This characteristic of goals (Elliott & Dweck, 1988) involves the achievement of a specific standard (e.g., "performance goals," e.g., lose 15 pounds) or the development of a specific skill ("learning goals," e.g., learn how to practice mindfulness meditation).

Instead of focusing on the end result, a *learning goal* focuses attention on the discovery of effective strategies to attain and sustain desired results (Seijts & Latham, 2006).

When trying to accomplish a learning goal, the individual will learn to master all the necessary skills that are associated with acquiring that goal. In the process, he or she may ask for feedback and reflect on progress in order to master whatever it takes to learn the new skill. On the other hand, trying to attain a specific performance goal can place additional demands on people, so much so that they may be unable to devote the necessary cognitive resources to mastering them.

Performance goals can be appropriate when the necessary skills to perform a task are already mastered and the primary focus is to exert more effort to reach a higher level of performance. Seigt & Latham (2006) found that individuals with learning goals demonstrated the following *advantages* over those with performance goals:

a) They took the time necessary to acquire the knowledge to perform the task effectively and to analyze the task-relevant information that was available to them.

b) They showed an increase in self-efficacy as a result of the discovery of appropriate strategies for task mastery. Other research supports the notion that learning goals are especially effective in enhancing self-efficacy and self-regulation (Schunk, 2001).

c) They had a higher commitment to their goals than did those with a performance goal. It is a good idea to set up goals that will allow your employees to focus on mastering the skills necessary to perform a new behavior as well as goals that target specific outcomes. For instance, a employee may have a performance goal of creating a more productive team or losing a specific amount of weight. By establishing a learning goal, the employee would focus on acquiring the skills to build a high performance team and to maintain a healthy weight.

5. *Avoidance vs. Approach Goals*

Goals that employees have can either be focused on securing desired outcomes (approach goals) but can also target avoiding unwanted outcomes (avoidance goals; e.g., Carver & Scheier, 1988). Avoidance goals as focused on eliminating an undesired end-state (e.g., "avoid being overly controlling in my staff meetings) but tend to have more ambiguous strategies associated with them and should typically be avoided.

Because *approach goals* tend to be more effective than most *avoidance goals*, one approach is to encourage employees to redefine any avoidance goals into approach goals (e.g., "be more participative and listen more to my staff during our meetings *before* I suggest my own ideas"). With some goals, employees may be able to use a "substitution goal" ("solicit input from others instead of expressing my own opinions") or a different goal for which the avoidance goal is instrumental ("seeking the ideas of others" is instrumental for "being seen as being a more involvement oriented leader").

Intentions are Good, But Good Intentions Are Bad

There is a large gap between intentions to change behavior and actual behaviors to change. Recent research suggests that attempts to change people's intentions alone *may not always result* in successful maintenance of behavior over time (Lawton, Conner, & McEachan, 2009). Many people express a strong desire and intent to become more effective and to try new behaviors, but often they never really initiate or sustain a new change for very long (e.g., relapse). Some recent evidence suggests that perceived importance and concern for the desired behavioral change endpoint might be the *best predictor* differentiating non-intenders from those who are successful adopters of new behavior, whereas *self-efficacy, perceived control, and being clear about the disadvantages*—the "cons"—of behavioral change are more important in discriminating successful maintainers from unsuccessful maintainers (Rhodes, Plotnikoff, & Courneya, 2008).

Why SMART Goals Aren't So Smart

We all know about "SMART" goals (the acronym has a variety of similar labels such as specific, measurable, attainable, relevant, and time bound). In a 2012 study, Leadership IQ, a leadership training and research company, studied 4,182 workers from 397 organizations to see what kind of goal-setting processes actually help employees achieve great things (Murphy, 2012). They discovered that people's goals *are not* particularly helpful. In fact, their survey found that *only 15%* of employees strongly agree that their goals helped the employees achieve great things. And only 13% of employees strongly agreed that their goals this year will help them maximize their full potential.

Several questions related to goals being measurable, realistic etc. had no unique predictive power in what employees actually achieved. To achieve success, people need to learn and practice new skills under specific situations over a long period of time until they switch from being consciously competent to unconscientiously competent. If SMART goals aren't the answer, then what is?

The Solution: Practice Plans

What you need to use with your employees is what psychologists call "*implementation intentions*" (i.e., habit triggers). We call this type of goal setting approach *Practice Plans* and they help convert goal intentions into deliberate practice under specific situations to form new habits. But, exactly what is it and does it really work?

Nearly *200 published studies* focusing on leadership, health, and interpersonal relations have shown that deciding in advance under what conditions your employee will plan to implement a new behavior can significantly increase their chances of actually doing it resulting in goal achievement. A meta-analysis involving over 8,000 participants in 94 independent studies revealed a medium-to-large effect size (d=0.65) of *Practice Plans* (implementation intentions) on goal success in a variety of domains (e.g. Interpersonal, environmental, health) on top of the effects of mere goal intentions (Gollwitzer, & Sheeran, 2006). Indeed, the use of *Practice Plans* appears to be very powerful way to help increase the likelihood of successful goal completion.

The Mechanics of Practice Plans

A '*Practice Plan*' is simply a plan in which your employee links a situation (opportunity to practice) with a specific behavior that is defined as a focus of the coaching engagement. To do this, all you have to do is reframe your employee's goals as "*if-then*" or "*when-then*" statements. The "if "or "when" part is the situational cue; the "then" part is your planned response or behavior to that cue. *Practice Plans* help facilitate ongoing practice of new behaviors until they become somewhat automatic (at least with 90 days of practice) and help to sustain these behaviors over time. *Practice Plans* help to facilitate the successful development of new habits.

Practice Plans work because research suggests that new habits are formed by actually practicing specific behaviors under situations and conditions that require a new response. Development of new skills is best supported by on-the-job experiences and feedback/coaching from others and often referred to as the *70-20-10 learning model* (first proposed in the 1980s by Center for Creative Leadership (CCL) authors and researchers Morgan McCall, Robert Eichinger and Michael Lombardo. The model states that learning occurs primarily from on-the-job experiences--70%, followed by learning from others--20% and, finally, from more passive courses /workshops--10%). Despite its popularity, there is little published research to actually support this exact ratio (Nowack, 2015).

To support the realization of goal intentions, most people also have a number of action items defined as single activities or tasks that support their learning and growth. In the example above ("Stay calm in stressful interpersonal situations"), a number of specific actions might be linked to this goal intention to support handling such stressors more effectively. Some examples might include watching a video on mindfulness meditation, reading an article or book on the topic or attending a class to learn the technique.

What is common about all of these action items is that they are *not necessarily ongoing* and can easily be "checked off" when completed. However, the successful completion of these action items does not necessarily equate to the successful learning of a new habit or ability to achieve the goal. In combination with *Practice Plans* these *Action Items* help an individual learn, apply and sustain new habits over time.

Indicators of Goal Progress

When people work toward goals, they monitor their progress in two ways --what they have achieved so far and how much they have left to do. It appears that individuals switch between the methods depending on how close they were to reaching their goal. Research with University students asked to pursue a specific goal (e.g., correcting errors in an essay) were less motivated halfway through the tasks, which likely reflects the point where they switch their focus from how much they got done to how much they had left to do. Additional research suggested that a shift in attention from the starting point to the end point occurred halfway through the task so this might be one of the most important times for consultants to follow-up with their employees (Bonezzi, Brendl, & De Angelis, 2011).

Personality Correlates with Goal Setting and Goal Pursuit

Naturally, individuals with different personality types will commit to their goals differently. Consultants should be aware of how their employees' personality traits will play a role in goal achievement. The reason it is important to understand this is because it can help consultants and employees establish goals that are realistic and suitable for a employee's personality type. The following traits have been associated with successful *goal attainment* in various research studies:

1. *Core Self-Evaluations (CSE)*

Judge, Locke, & Durham (1997) defined core self-evaluations as basic conclusions or bottom-line evaluations individuals hold that constitute a higher order construct of one's self-concept. Core self-evaluations are composed of four personality traits: self-esteem, generalized self-efficacy, emotional stability (low neuroticism), and locus of control (Erez & Judge, 2001). In other words, the more an individual typifies the core self-evaluation traits, the more likely he or she is to attain the goals he or she sets out to achieve. For example, people with low self-efficacy are unlikely to choose or commit to an ambitious goal, whereas people with high self-efficacy not only commit to ambitious goals, but set even more ambitious ones once they've reached their initial goals (Latham & Locke, 2008).

2. *Psychological Capital*

Recent empirical evidence that *psychological capital* can be used to explain how employees are motivated to acquire, maintain and foster the necessary resources to attain successful performance outcomes (Peterson, Luthans, Avolio, Walumbwa & Zhang, 2011). Specifically, an individual's motivation and choices towards goal initiation and completion can be explained by four psychological resources that in-clude self-efficacy, hope, optimism and resilience which in turn affect both motivation and performance.

Psychological capital has been defined as having more measurement stability than emotional states, but not as stable as personality consisting of four psychological resources that increase the probability of success based on motivated effort, persistence and goal attainment/performance (Peterson et al., 2011).

The first component of this higher-order core construct is *self-efficacy* which is defined as the confidence and belief about one's abilities to motivate both internal and external resources to execute tasks and contribute to high performance. Second, is *hope* which is defined as a positive motivational state that facilitates goal directed energy and success. Third, is *optimism,* which is defined as an explanatory style that helps interpret negative and positive events in a way to optimize goal success as well as a positive orientation towards the future. Fourth is *resilience* which is defined as the ability to bounce back from failure or challenges. Psychological capital has been demonstrated to be a significant predictor of job performance and work success and may be changed based on developmental interventions, repeated feedback from leaders, peers or even the job itself (Peterson et al., 2011).

3. *Perfectionism*

Some people set goals that are truly *impossible* for them to attain. They may, nevertheless, persist in pursuing such goals because their self-worth (self-esteem) is contingent upon goal attainment (Latham & Locke, 2008). People who are perfectionists might set unreasonable goals or be unwilling to back off and quit, despite clear signs that the goal is unattainable.

4. *Conscientiousness/Drive*

Achievement striving, dependable, and conscientious individuals are more likely to set and achieve their goals (Barrick, Mount, & Strauss, 1993). Since conscientiousness is related to traits such as organization, persistence, and purposefulness, these traits are similar to the need for determination, deliberation, caution, and reliability, which are necessary for goal achievement. Research shows that personality variables, such as conscientiousness, are related to goal level, self-efficacy, and performance (Mitchell, Thompson, & Falvy, 2000). Conscientious individuals are highly meticulous, detail-oriented, and driven, so they are more likely to put forth the appropriate effort to enact and sustain change.

There is also a growing recognition and support linking the personality factor of conscientiousness with health/disease processes, health-related goals and behaviors and longevity (Bogg & Roberts, 2013). In general, conscientious individuals tend to find stress-related situations less demanding than less conscientious individuals allowing them to avoid relapse and return to old habits and behaviors once they have set goals. Overall, conscientiousness as a relatively stable pattern of individual differences to follow norms for impulse control, to delay gratification, to be organized, follow rules and be goal-directed would appear to play an important role in both goal initiation and pursuit.

Consultants should become familiar with a number of valid, brief, and cost-free assessments instrument (e.g., www.innateindex.com) for measuring conscientiousness as many do not always use conscientiousness as a label or conceptual framework. A good source of various measures of conscientiousness for consultants is the website by Dr. Brent Roberts at the University of Illinois: http://faculty.las.illinois.edu/bwroberts/conscientiousness/ index.html

5. *Grit*

"Grit" is a trait that is based on an individual's passion for a particular long-term goal or a particular end state of a goal. Individuals who are "gritty" often have a powerful motivation to achieve their objectives (Duckworth, Peterson, Mathews, & Kelly, 2007). Measurement of "grit" includes items that tap into both perseverance of effort as well as strength of interests or passion. This type of employee would tend to set long-term goals and not be deterred by setbacks, initial failures, or ongoing challenges. As such, individuals high in Grit are able to maintain their determination and motivation over long periods of time despite experiences with failure and adversity.

6. *Mood*

Research indicates that "one's mood at the moment can influence goal choice" (Mitchell et al., 2000). Thus, people with a more positive mood may report higher confidence levels and, as a result, set more challenging goals. Additional research suggests that when individuals are in a bad mood, they tend to fixate their energy on their negative affect over cognitive and behavioral efforts towards attaining their goals (Gollwitzer & Sheeran, 2006).

> ## Factoid: When Stressed, People Revert to Old Habits (Even Good Ones)
>
> Researchers followed student eating, exercise and study habits and found that when they were stressed and sleep deprived they were more likely to stick to old habits (Neal, Wood, & Drolet, 2013). For example, students who ate unhealthy during the semester ate even worse during exams. Those with healthy eating habits or those who worked out regularly exercised regularly and ate especially well while under pressure.

Asking Employees about Future Predictions of Behavior to *Increase* Implementation Intentions

There is considerable evidence that repetitive behaviors (both unhealthy and healthy) are very difficult to change, even when people intend to do so (Webb & Sheeran, 2006). Therefore, methods to strengthen or disrupt behavior repetition would appear to be beneficial to sustaining desirable change over time. Current research suggests that asking questions regarding future behavior can lead to significant changes in that behavior (Chandon, Smith, Morowitz, Spangenberg, & Sprott, 2011).

When asked to make predictions about future behavior, people think about what they normally do (past behavior) and what they think they should do (personal norms). In one experiment, Chandon and colleagues (2011) asked college students to predict whether they would read books or watch the news in the next week. Compared to a control group, students asked to predict their behavior were more likely to repeat what they had done the week before. Asking about future exercising led students who had only exercised for 10 minutes in the week before to exercise for an estimated 94 additional minutes in the next week (an increase of 138 percent).

Apparently, when people have set targets about how much they should engage in a behavior for themselves, asking them to predict whether they will engage in that behavior in the next week makes them think about what they should do and increases the likelihood of implementing their intention. However, asking questions led to an estimated 23 fewer minutes of exercising (a decrease of 11 percent) among those who had exercised for 150 minutes in the week before.

When personal norms are weak or not accessible at the time of the prediction request, asking people about their future behavior strengthens behavior repetition. People become more likely to repeat what they normally do. However, when personal norms are strong or made accessible at the time of the prediction request, behavior prediction appears to actually weaken behavior repetition. People become less likely to repeat what they normally do.

Factoid: Nearly Half of Our Daily Behavior is Habitual

A study by Wendy Wood and David Neal at Duke University (2007) asked people to record what they were doing, thinking, and feeling for one hour for several days in a row. About 47 percent of the behaviors that participants listed in their diaries tended to be repeated in the same physical location almost every day (i.e., almost half of what people do are based on habits we have formed). Furthermore, they found that when participants in the study changed their environments (e.g., moved or transferred to a new school), habit performance was disrupted and behavior was less automatic and under intentional control. Indeed, as Aristotle said, "we are what we repeatedly do."

Figure 4-1

The Twelve Rules of Goal Pursuit Success

1	*Goal intentions* are weakly associated with actual long-term behavior change but practice plans (i.e., *habit triggers*) significantly increase goal achievement (Gollwitzer & Sheeran, 206; Nowack & Mashihi, 2012).
2	Motivation is at the lowest point in the *middle* of goal pursuits so this is the most important time for coaches to follow-up with their clients (Bonezzi, Brendl, & De Angelis, 2011).
3	Challenging and even unrealistic goals actually inspire, rather than, compromise goal accomplishment (Linde, Jeffrey, Finch, Ng. & Rothman, 2004).
4	Trying to change a behavior or a new habit forever is *not* the best strategy—fixed periods allow people to adjust their strategies (Locke & Latham, 1990).
5	Expectations from others and external rewards are less effective for successful behavior change than *intrinsic* motivation and rewards (Pelletier, Dion, Slovinec-D'Angelo, & Reid, 2004).
6	Trying hard to *resist temptation* leads to worse goal performance and make goal failure more likely (Wegner, 2009; Hagger et al., 2010).
7	*Mastery* goals (those that focus on acquisition of knowledge and skills) are far superior to successful pursuit and accomplishment than *performance* based goals (e.g., losing weight; Elliot & Dweck, 1988).
8	The shift from conscious competence to *unconscious competence* takes, on average, about 90 days of deliberate and varied practice for complex behaviors (e.g., learning to practice mindfulness meditation; Lally et al., 2009).
9	To become the "best of the best" requires, on average, 10 years or 10,000 hours of *deliberate and varied practice* (Ericcson, 1996).
10	People *high* in the personality trait called conscientiousness (i.e., those disciplined, organized, achievement oriented, goal focused) are *significantly* more likely to be successful in the completion of goals (Bogg & Roberts, 2013; Rhodes & Smith, 2008).
11	*Small wins* and minor steps forward have the most significant impact on the *positive emotions* we feel towards goal pursuits (Amabile & Kramer, 2011).
12	*Quitting* goals that are unattainable may cause better health compared to those who persevere and push themselves to succeed in the face of constant failure (Miller & Wrosch).

Chapter 9:
Facilitating Goal Implementation

> Motivation is what gets you started. Habit is
> what keeps you going.
>
> ### JIM ROHN

Once goals have been set, achieving them requires persistence, the proper techniques, social support, and preventative measures that help avoid relapse. This chapter will review what can go *wrong* in implementing goals and in strategies for sustaining them.

Ingredients for Learning a New Behavior

There is, in fact, a big difference between those who possess expertise vs. those who are expert in what they do. In *The Cambridge Handbook of Expertise and Expert Performance*, a recent book co-edited by Anders Ericsson (2006), the authors conclude that great performance comes mainly from two things:

- Regularly *obtaining* concrete and constructive *feedback*
- *Deliberate practice*

Ericsson and others use the phrase "deliberate practice" to mean focused, structured, serious, and detailed attempts to get better. Deliberate practice has to be challenging and difficult. As it turns out, expert performance requires about 10 years, or approximately 10,000 to 20,000 hours of deliberate practice. Little evidence exists for expert performance before *10 years of deliberate practice in any field* (Ericsson, 1996) and recent research suggests that sheer number of hours engaged in practice is not as important as the quality of deliberate practice Ericsson, 2013)

Factoid: Practice Doesn't Make Perfect

Two authors of Cambridge Handbook of Expertise and Expert Performance analyzed the diaries of 24 elite figure skaters to determine what might explain some of their performance success. They found that the best skaters spent 68 percent of their practice performing very hard jumps and routines, compared to those who were less successful, who spent about 48 percent of their time doing the same difficult things.

Recent research by Phillippa Lally and colleagues from the U.K. suggests that new behaviors can become automatic after, on average *18 to 254* days, but it depends on the complexity of the behavior you are trying to put into place and your personality (Lally, 2009). Lally and her colleagues studied volunteers who chose to change an eating, drinking, or exercise behavior and tracked them for success. These volunteers completed a self-report diary, which they entered on a Web site log. They were asked to try the new behavior each day for 84 days. For the habits, 27 chose an eating behavior, 31 a drinking behavior, 34 an exercise behavior, and four did something else, like practicing meditation.

Analysis of these behaviors indicated that it took 66 days, on average, for a new behavior to become automatic and a new "habit" to seem natural. The range was anywhere from 18 to 254 days. The mean number of days varied by the complexity of the habit:

1. Drinking averaged about 59 days
2. Eating averaged about 65 days
3. Exercise averaged about 91 days

This study does suggest that it can take a *large number of repetitions* by a person for a new behavior to become a habit.

Therefore, creating new habits requires tremendous self-control to be maintained for a significant period of time before these habits become automatic, and performed without any real self-control. For example, think about how much time you spend consciously operating your car when you are driving. For most people, it takes about *three months of constant practice* before a more complicated, new behavior gets set in our neural pathways as something we are comfortable with and something that is seemingly automatic. Adopting a new physical workout routine or learning to become a more participative leader might take a great deal of practice before becoming a habit.

The Neuroscience of "Practice" and Learning a New Behavior

In addition to an individual's self-control, discipline, and the time spent in forming a habit, research has indicated that mentally focusing on practicing a new behavior can contribute greatly to learning a new behavior. Harvard University neuroscientist, Alvaro Pascual-Leone conducted an experiment on how humans practice by comparing mentally practicing a task with physically practicing a task. He experimented with a group of individuals that spent five days learning to play piano for two hours each day. They were instructed to play piano as fluidly as they could by trying to keep up with the metronome's 60 beats per minute. At the end of each day's practice session, they sat beneath a coil of wire that sent a brief magnetic pulse into the motor cortex of their brain.

This transcranial-magnetic-stimulation (TMS) test revealed how much of the motor cortex controlled the finger movements needed for the piano exercise. When the scientists compared the TMS data on the two groups, they found that those who actually played the piano and those who only imagined doing so resulted in the following: The region of motor cortex that controls the piano-playing movement of fingers also expanded in the brains of volunteers who imagined playing the music, just as it had in those who had actually played it (Pascual-Leon, Amedi, Fregni, Lotfi, & Merabet, 2005).

Figure 9-2

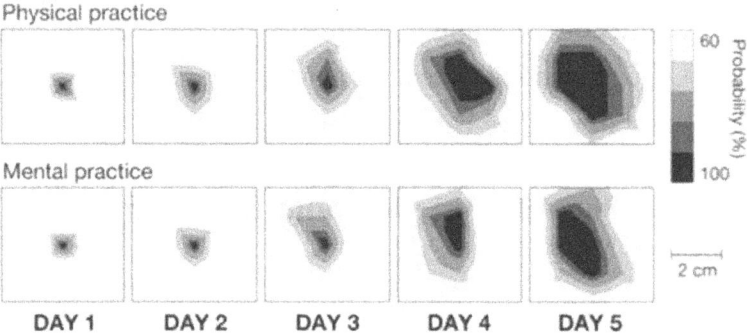

Figure 9-2 illustrates the following:

1. Comparison of a mental practice group on the piano versus a physical practice group (both two hours per day for five days) showed nearly similar changes in cortical pathways

2. Mental practice, plus two hours of physical practice, resulted in equal performance at the end of the five-day study period

Additionally, Tartaglia, Bamert, Mast, & Herzog (2009) conducted research on "mental imagery" and found that perceptual learning can occur by mentally visualizing an act of a behavior as much as it can occur via the physical action of the actual behavior. In other words, they suggest that *thinking about something repeatedly* could be as good as doing it. In a series of experiments, the researchers asked some participants to practice identifying which line in a series of three parallel lines a central line was closest to and to identify it by pushing the correct button. In follow-up post-training exercises, these participants improved their baseline performance significantly. The other group of participants, who instead were asked to *imagine* the bisecting line's proximity, improved their performance significantly. Therefore, training through imagery was actually sufficient for perceptual learning.

These findings provide important implications for learning new habits and behaviors. Perhaps in addition to spending time physically practicing a new behavior, employees can also devote time to *being mindful* and imagining their success at learning a new task.

The Four Stages of Learning a New Behavior

When implementing goals, it is important to understand the process by which individuals learn a new behavior. Abraham Maslow posits that there are four stages to achieving competence and eventually mastering a new behavior. According to his model, *learning is the process that moves from incompetence to competence.*

Think of something in your own life that you learned how to do really well: driving a car, riding a bike, skiing, etc. Once you have learned how to do this, it becomes automatic; you rarely think about the activity anymore. Between not knowing that something needs to be learned and mastering a skill, every individual undergoes four stages of learning:

Figure 9-3

Coaching and Behavior Change Model

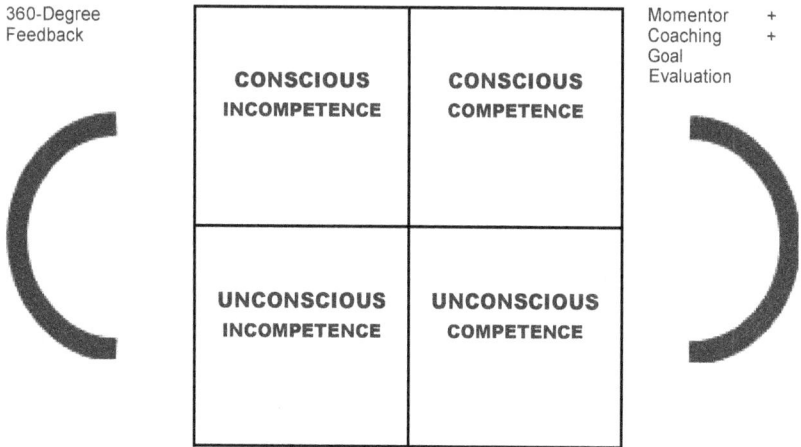

360-Degree Feedback			Momentor + Coaching + Goal Evaluation
	CONSCIOUS INCOMPETENCE	CONSCIOUS COMPETENCE	
	UNCONSCIOUS INCOMPETENCE	UNCONSCIOUS COMPETENCE	

1. **Unconscious Incompetence**: *"I don't know what I don't know."*

The individual neither understands nor knows how to do something, nor recognizes this deficit. During this stage, the employee is unaware that his or her behavior needs to change. The coach finds ways to assess the employee in order to provide feedback.

2. **Conscious Incompetence**: *"Now, I know what I didn't know."*

Though the individual does not understand or know how to do something, he or she recognizes the deficit, without yet addressing it. During this stage, the employee receives feedback and understands the need to take on a new set of behaviors. The employee may receive feedback on his or her performance, and gets ready to begin learning a new behavior.

3. **Conscious Competence**: *"I know what I know."*

The individual understands or knows how to do something. However, demonstrating that skill or knowledge requires a great deal of consciousness and concentration. At some point, the employee begins to realize a certain level of mastery with his or her behavior. The employee may not be an expert, but knows that he or she has some expertise. For instance, say the employee is trying to learn how to become an active listener. He or she may realize that it's easy to listen when not being criticized. This insight facilitates practice to actively listen to people even if they are providing criticism.

4. **Unconscious Competence**: *"I'm not aware of what I know."*

The individual has had so much practice with a skill that it has become "second nature" and can be performed easily (often without concentrating too deeply). He or she may be able to teach it to others, depending upon how and when it was learned. For example, after driving a car for a few years to a certain destination, a driver may not even be aware of how he or she arrived there because the same route has been taken so many times that it has become automatic.

Factoid: Stuck in the Middle

When people work toward goals, they monitor their progress in two ways; what they have achieved so far and how much they have left to do. It appears that individuals switch between the methods depending on how close they were to reaching their goal. Research with University students asked to pursue a specific goal (e.g., correcting errors in an essay) were less motivated halfway through the tasks, which likely reflects the point where they switch their focus from how much they got done to how much they had left to do.

Additional research suggested that a shift in attention from the starting point to the end point occurred halfway through the tasks, so this might be one of the most important times for consultants to follow-up with their employees (Bonezzi, Brendl, & De Angelis, 2011).

Chapter 10:
Measuring Goal Progress

Life is change. Growth is optional. Choose wisely.

KAREN KAISER CLARK

Defining a Way to Measure Success

Evaluating an individual's progress at achieving goals is critical to the success of goal attainment. There are various ways consultants and employees can track, monitor, and evaluate progress. The measurement process will vary, depending on the type of employees and their needs. For example, a manager in an organization may participate in annual performance reviews, whereas a employee seeking health and wellness may utilize tools that monitor his or her stress levels.

1. **Annual Performance Reviews**

   Employees working in organizations that provide annual reviews can utilize this form of feedback despite some obvious limitations of appraisal systems today (Collins & Bell, 2013; Culbuert & Rout, 2010). Ongoing feedback about performance by one's manager may be better to provide a metric around goal achievement and success.

2. **Performance Conversations**

   Employees working in organizations can ask their co-workers or colleagues for feedback. It is a good idea to ask the opinions of those that have direct contact with the employees. Employees can also seek the feedback of family and peers. Oftentimes, close individuals will be able to determine change and progress. It is a good idea to seek feedback from those individuals they trust.

3. Team Feedback

If an individual is part of a group or work team or even leads a team, it is a great opportunity to ask questions for better feedback. Because each team member has a slightly different perspective, gathering feedback from all colleagues on a team might accurately clarify strengths and potential development areas. In addition, the process of asking for feedback can lead to better rapport and trust in relationships.

4. "Pulse" Surveys of Goal Progress

The purpose of "pulse" surveys is to continue monitoring progress and new areas for development. "Pulse" surveys are a simple and efficient way to measure behavioral change. They are short and focus only on the behavioral goal. They are designed to help consultants track performance in small increments.

An Envisia Learning, Inc. product called *Momentor* is an example of a tool to measure and assess goal progress and effectiveness. Participants are able to ask other raters to provide specific feedback on whether others have noticed increased effectiveness and improvement based on their development plan efforts resulting in a brief "progress pulse" evaluation report (www.envisialearning.com/momentor).

Goal: Acknowledge Ideas from Others

Initiated May 23, 2014   **(6 raters were invited, 6 responded)** Show Raters

Compare to: January 25, 2014   :

Ratings Distribution

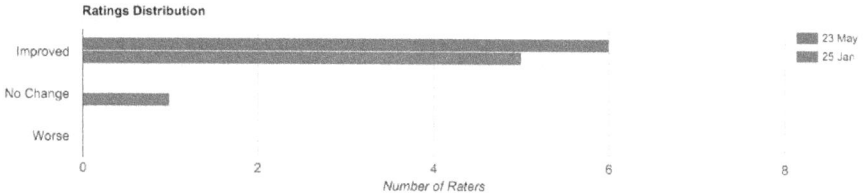

Sally Mentor left the following feedback:
"*Peers and seniors observed the change and commented on it positively, so it is clear that previous behavior was observed and change is noticeable and appreciated!*"

Experiential Techniques

Reading books, listening to podcasts and attending seminars may be useful, but current research suggests that successful behavioral change can be facilitated much more rapidly and deeply by using more active group and experiential approaches, such as work sample simulations, case studies, and on-the-job activities (e.g., special projects, stretch assignments, etc.). For example, in our coaching practice, when we assess employees through video assessment role-plays, we find a tremendous amount of specific detail about our employees' progress. Using experiential techniques can help our employees assess their current level of proficiency and skills and point out additional areas for them to consider working to enhance their effectiveness.

5. Reminders ("Professional Nagging")

Reminders have been widely used as tools to help facilitate behavioral change and have been extensively studied in both health psychology and behavioral medicine literature (Fung, Woods,

Asch, Glassman, & Doebbeling, 2004). Reminders to employees and patients in the form of e-mails, text messages, phone calls, and other tools appear to be particularly effective in improving an adherence to new behaviors and preventing relapse. Consultants should utilize the full range of reminder tools and techniques with their employees to help them focus on practicing and sustaining new behaviors. Some vendors also offer automated reminder systems (e.g., *Momentor* by Envisia Learning, Inc., provides e-mail and/or text message reminders about their goal progress to employees who have created their online development plans). The most effective consultants seem to be positive "professional nags" for their employees, encouraging them to stay on course with the implementation of their goals.

There are also numerous free or inexpensive internet-based or Smart Phone apps and calendar systems that provide text and e-mail reminders that can be creatively used. Consultants can make recommendations on which system might be best, based on their employee's interest and behavioral goals.

Tracking and Monitoring Progress

What do you think is the *top motivator* of performance for individuals at all levels? If you thought it was recognition, rewards, incentives, interpersonal support, specific feedback, or clarity of goals, you would be wrong. Teresa Amabile and Stephen Kramer (2010) completed a multi-year study tracking the day-to-day activities, emotions, and motivational drives of over 600 managers in diverse settings to determine what really motivates workers.

The number one drive for motivation was making progress or headway on goals and work activities. In Amabile and Kramer's research, days when individuals reported making headway in their jobs, or days when they received support that helped them overcome obstacles, their emotions were the most positive and their level of satisfaction was highest. On days when they felt they were "spinning their wheels" or experiencing barriers to meaningful accomplishment, their emotions, moods, and motivations were significantly lower.

Being *able to see progress* is a *key* to sustaining motivation to continue with the goals, tasks, and activities that have been initiated. Systems for tracking, monitoring, and evaluating progress on goals can serve as useful mechanisms to reduce lapses and relapses with new behaviors. For example, Envisia's online goal setting and reminder system *Momentor* is designed to provide a visual tracking and monitoring system to help employees see the progress they are making. Based on the research of Amabile and Kramer, such tracking systems should help employees stay on track to complete goals and specific action plans.

Create a Goal For: Leadership/Influence

← Go Back & Select Another Goal

Step 1: Finalize Your Goal

Define your specific, achievable, and measurable goal in terms of what behavioral outcomes you would like to see if you are successful

(Examples: "Control my emotions in stressful situations" or "Be more participative with my direct reports and involve them more in problem solving, planning and decision making situations")

> ### Solicits Input and Involves Staff in Decision Making, Problem Solving and Planning Processes

Step 2: Due Dates and Progress

When do you think progress on this goal is noticeable to you and/or others? (Required)

-- Please select -- ˅ month(s)

When would like to accomplish this goal by (Optional):

Step 3: Share Your Progress

We highly recommend that you share your progress with people you think could help encourage you to achieve this goal. In Momentor, we call these people "Goal Mentors".

We keep goal mentors in the loop by sending them an email every time either you or your coach (if you are working with one):

- Achieve or discuss this goal
- Add, complete or discuss Action Items
- Add or discuss Practice Plans (we'll teach you about these later)

There are a few activities that goal mentors will **not** be updated on. These are:

- Add, update or discuss goal mentors
- Request, receive or discuss goal feedback

Keep my manager, or anyone else, informed of my progress (Optional):

☑ Yes, email: Rater1 Test1 rater1@envisiaonline.com

[Save]

We will notify your coaches (Andy Parkinson, Ken Nowack, Ken Nowack and Sandra Sample) that you created this goal.

Factoid: 50% of our Time is Spent Desiring Things and 20% Resisting a Desire

A field study used personal assistant devices to prompt 205 adults with a desire-related questionnaire on 7 random times per day for a period of one week. Extrapolating results to a 16 hour waking day, if you beeped a random person 100 times during that period, he or she would, on average, report currently desiring things on 50 of those occasions, trying to resist a current desire on 20 of those occasions, and giving in to temptation on about 3 of those occasions (Hofmann, Vohs, & Baumeister, 2012).

Chapter 11:
Relapse Prevention

> If at first you don't succeed, then skydiving
> definitively isn't for you.

> ## STEVEN WRIGHT

For most people, willpower and determination alone aren't enough for sustaining new behaviors that are healthy or changing old ones that are potentially damaging. Consultants should educate their employees that *relapse* is a normal part of most behavioral change processes. They can educate their employees about what leads to these "lapses" and how to effectively cope with periods of personal stress that will enable them to continue to grow and learn over time without totally relapsing back to old entrenched behaviors and habits.

Principles of relapse prevention include identifying high-risk situations for relapse (like a change in season) and developing appropriate solutions (like finding a place to walk inside during the winter). Helping people distinguish between a *lapse* (e.g., a few days of not participating in a planned activity) and a *relapse* (e.g., an extended period of not participating) is thought to improve adherence.

How Does Relapse Occur?

Marlatt & Gordon (1985) created the Relapse Prevention model that provides a set of cognitive-behavioral strategies to prevent or limit relapse. A central aspect of the model is the detailed classification of factors or situations that can precipitate relapse or contribute to such episodes. While much of this research is geared toward addictive behaviors, the concepts surrounding relapse prevention can be applied to all types of behavioral change interventions. Research suggests that a number of specific factors contributing to relapse include the following:

1. **Negative emotional states:** Anger, anxiety, depression, frustration, and boredom are emotional states that are associated with the highest rates of relapse (Marlatt & Gordon, 1985).

2. **Situations that involve another person or group of people:** Interpersonal situations like conflict can trigger relapse.

3. **Social pressure:** Being around individuals who model employees' old habits can trigger relapse (e.g., attending a party where many people are smoking and drinking when seeking to quit).

4. **Positive emotional states:** An employee who drinks may be more likely to revert to old habits during a celebration.

Factoid: Five Hours of Temptation

According to psychologist, Saul Shiffman, the number one predictor of behavior lapses is emotional: the level of negative affect during the four to five hours leading up to the lapse (e.g., anger, anxiety, depression, or a bad mood that ramps up over a period of hours).

Employees' reactions or responses to different situations can trigger relapse. However, an employee that can execute effective coping strategies is less likely to relapse, compared to a person who is lacking those skills. Consultants must teach employees to anticipate the possibility of relapse and to recognize and cope with situations that can trigger each individual differently. They can help their employee's awareness of cognitive, behavioral, and emotional reactions in order to prevent a lapse from escalating into a relapse

(Marlatt, 1999).

Relapse Prevention Strategies for Consultants

1. *Identifying and Coping with High Risk Situations:* In order to anticipate and plan for situations that trigger employees to revert back to old habits, the employee must first identify the different situations in which he or she may experience difficulty coping. These situations can be identified through the coaching process and through various assessment processes.

2. *Enhancing Self-Efficacy:* Marlatt (1999) recommend preventing relapse by the use of strategies designed to increase an employee's sense of mastery and sense of being able to handle difficult situations without lapsing. They recommend an emphasis on collaboration between the employee and therapist or coach.

3. *Eliminating Myths:* It is important for consultants to counteract the misperceptions about a employee's current behavior. For instance, thinking that smoking is "not that bad" and helps release stress is a myth that an individual may hold in order to keep him or her from altering his or her behavior. Or a manager who believes that micromanagement is what helped his or her employees become productive may hold an inaccurate belief that needs to be shifted into reality. The coach's role is to help employees understand these misperceptions and provide them with accurate information about the consequences of their behaviors.

4. *Lapse Management:* According to research, "despite precautions and preparations, many employees committed to abstinence will experience a lapse after initiating abstinence" (Larimer, Palmer, & Marlatt, 1999, p. 151). This notion holds

true for any behavior that is an addiction or even a regular habit. Lapse-management strategies focus on halting the lapse and combating the abstinence violation effect to preventing an uncontrolled relapse episode. The coach and employee can discuss a "lapse management plan" that includes all the different steps the employee can take to get back on track in progress and development.

5. ***Cognitive Restructuring:*** This concept is also known as "Reframing" (as discussed in the *Encourage* section). It is used to assist employees in modifying their attributions for and perceptions of the relapse process. Specifically, consultants can train employees to reframe their perceptions of lapses and not to view them as failures, but as signals to alter or increase the plan to cope more effectively.

One way of doing this would be to eliminate "black-and-white thinking". According to Larimer, et al., (1999), black-and-white thinking can turn a minor lapse into a major one. After a small slip, many people simply give up because they believe one failure means they don't have the ability to change. This "abstinence-violation effect" is the belief that anything less than perfection is a total failure. It leads the quitter to conclude that they just don't have the willpower to succeed (McGowen, 2010).

It is important for consultants to educate employees about the process of relapse prevention. Behavioral change is a process, and relapse is an inevitable part of the journey. Despite the occurrence of relapse, employees should also be aware that they *can* actually improve. In fact, it is suggested that if handled the right way, a relapse can actually be an opportunity for lasting behavioral change. It provides opportunity to develop and improve techniques for anticipating and overcoming bad habits (McGowen, 2010).

Chapter 12:
Building a Support Group

> Live in such a way that you would not be ashamed to sell your parrot to the town gossip.
>
> ## WILL ROGERS

Individuals seeking to change behaviors and sustain those changes may need the support of professionals, peers, friends, or family members to help sustain momentum. Professional help, family support, and planning are required just as much as a desire and commitment to change. Consultants can refer employees to groups or associations that focus on an individual's growth. These groups can provide those individuals with support and a network of others that can relate to them.

Many researchers have found evidence that suggests social support is a promising technique for promoting healthy behavioral change. They suggest that social support is more effective when two individuals have similar characteristics or issues (Center of Excellence for Training and Research Translation, 2008). For example, a recent study on the effect of support groups on individuals seeking to quit smoking suggests that positive and negative support are both important factors in the early phase of quitting, but it is the continued minimization of negative support that predicts the maintenance of nonsmoking (Lawhon, Humfleet, Hall, Reus, & Munoz, 2009).

Types of Social Support to Facilitate Successful Behavioral Change

The following are common sources of networking and social

support that can help foster behavioral change, both at work and away from the job:

- **Family, Friends, and Peers**: Peers, family members, friends, and networking groups all contribute to sticking through change plans. On the other hand, if family members, friends, and peers do not support change efforts, individuals may be more prone to relapse. For example, if a smoking addict is surrounded by friends that smoke, he or she is exposed to a "high-risk" situation that can hinder efforts to quit smoking.

- **Consultants and Counselors:** Without the help of a coach or counselor, employees may have a harder time overcoming change. Consultants should ensure that employees have the proper support to overcome challenges and sustain change.

- **Organizational Support:** Employees within organizations can utilize the support of their colleagues, mentors, peers, human resource personnel, and managers. While the support of these individuals depends on the organizational culture and its receptivity to change efforts, it is still useful to seek someone in an organization that can act as a "role model" to change efforts.

- **Specialized Support Groups:** There are various support groups that have been demonstrated to be effective for individuals seeking change. Individuals of similar circumstances meet either monthly, weekly, or during weekend-long events to discuss and share experiences with change efforts. Such groups include self-discovery programs, leadership programs, business retreats, spiritual courses, addiction and recovery centers, etc. These groups can be particularly helpful in that people can learn from the experiences of one another and gain a sense of belonging.

- **On-line Goal Setting and Tracking Systems:** Beyond social networking sites, there are online tools that can essentially act as online consultants. For instance, Envisia Learning's goal setting and evaluation platform called Momentor provides recommendations for change, tracks improvements, and provides various accountability systems to ensure behavioral goal progress (www.envisialearning.com).

The Benefits of a Social Support Network

Numerous studies have demonstrated that having a network of supportive relationships contributes to psychological well-being. Having a social support network can be beneficial in the following ways:

- **Sense of Belonging.** Often times, individuals feel they are alone in the change process. However, being surrounded by others that are going through similar circumstances, can help them feel part of an entity where their challenges and growth opportunities is perceived as common.
- **Increased Sense of Self-Worth.** Being around individuals to connect and exchange support with can be gratifying and increase a sense of self-value.
- **Feelings of Security.** A social network provides employees with access to information, advice, guidance, and other types of assistance, should employees need them. Employees can feel understood and safe when they have individuals that can be of help or have similar circumstances. In addition, individuals have an easier time opening up about their challenges when they are surrounded by others that can empathize with them.
- **Sustaining Development.** When employees are surrounded by individuals that can support their progress, they may be less likely to lapse back into old habits.

Avoiding "Toxic" Individuals

Oftentimes, employees have a difficult time sustaining progress because of the individuals around them. It is very important for employees undergoing change efforts not to surround themselves with individuals that trigger emotional stress and lead them toward high-risk relapse situations. A coach should assess employees' environment and set boundaries around those individuals that are likely to be influential in a toxic way.

Engineering Social Networking Online

With the growth of online social networking in people's lives, it would seem convenient for individuals to utilize online networking sites for support. Existing online peer groups or the creation of virtual support groups is common (Center of Excellence for Training and Research Translation, 2008). Popular social sites like Twitter, Facebook, LinkedIn, Google+, etc., can also be tools to build a social coalition with individuals that face similar situations. For instance, a leader that is seeking to work better with his or her employees may look to particular blogs and posts on one of the online sites that provides a network of individuals that share blogs, articles, thoughts, advice, and questions, through postings and chat rooms.

Chapter 13:
Approaches to Developing Talent

Success comes from knowing that you did your best to become the best that you are capable of becoming.

JOHN WOODEN

Developing talent at all levels of an organization is critical to facilitate retention and engagement and to remain globally competitive. However, "The Coaching Conundrum 2009: Building a coaching culture that drives organizational success," a recent survey by Blessing White, Inc., revealed that about 84 percent of all managers are expected to coach talent, but only 52 percent actually do (only 39 percent in Europe), and only 24 percent are rewarded or recognized for coaching and developing talent.

Managers and internal consultants should consider a variety of ways to develop talent, including focusing on activities, assignments, and work-related projects to enhance knowledge, skills, and experience. These might include:

- Start-up Assignments
- Fix-it Assignments
- Stretch Assignments
- Professional Development, Mentoring, or Coaching
- Non-Work Activities

Figure 4-6 summarizes some suggestions for activities, tasks, and assignments designed to support talent development at all levels of the organization. These behavior-based activities are likely to be more powerful than just attending internal workshops or taking self-directed online webinars or programs. Of course, most organizations will put more energy into their *high-potential and high-performing* talent than those who are poor performers or who have serious personality and skill deficits making them high risk for potential "derailment."

Figure 4-6

Activities, Tasks, and Assignments to Support Talent Development

Activity, Task or Assignment	Examples
Start-Up Assignments These activities, tasks, and assignments emphasize leadership, delegation, problem solving and decision making skills, learning new content quickly, working under time pressures, and working collaboratively with groups of people.	1. Chair a task force on a business problem. 2. Go off-site to troubleshoot problems or improve processes. 3. Install a new system, program, or procedure. 4. Initiate a large-scale change project within the organization. 5. Plan an off-site meeting, conference, or convention. 6. Serve on a new project or product review committee. 7. Work on a short-term international start-up initiative.
Fix-It Assignments These activities, tasks, and assignments emphasize team building, individual responsibility, dealing effectively with different people including executives, peers and direct reports. These assignments may require being responsible for dealing with a specific crisis where conflict is likely.	1. Manage a group of inexperienced people. 2. Manage a dysfunctional team. 3. Resolve conflict among subordinates. 4. Manage a group of low-competence and low-performing talent. 5. Assign a challenging project that failed previously. 6. Close down a department, unit, or failing business.
Stretch Assignments These activities, tasks, and assignments emphasize intellectual challenge, problem analysis and influencing skills. In many cases, individuals taking on these assignments may lack experience or skills in some areas.	1. Conduct a competitive analysis. 2. Create a strategic plan for a department. 3. Conduct a market analysis with recommendations for gaining market share. 4. Coordinate a process improvement initiative. 5. Chair or participate in a cross-functional team.
Professional Development or Mentoring These activities, tasks, and assignments emphasize learning, training, mentoring, and coaching.	1. Teach someone how to do something they are not an expert in. 2. Seek an external executive coach. 3. Seek and utilize an internal or external mentor. 4. Work with a senior leader who is particularly successful.
Non-Work Activities These activities, tasks, and assignments take place away from work and emphasize individual leadership, contribution to a cause, and working with new people.	1. Join a community board. 2. Become active in a volunteer organization. 3. Work with a charitable organization. 4. Become active in a professional association in a leadership role.

Envisia Learning Inc. Performance Coaching Model

The use of a *performance coaching model* can provide managers and consultants with a framework to enhance the skills and productivity of talent at all levels of the organization. This performance-based coaching model helps to clarify contracting, the definition of specific goals, typical assessments to be used, and approaches to maximize both individual goals and organizational outcomes.

Figure 4-7
Envisia Learning Performance Coaching Model

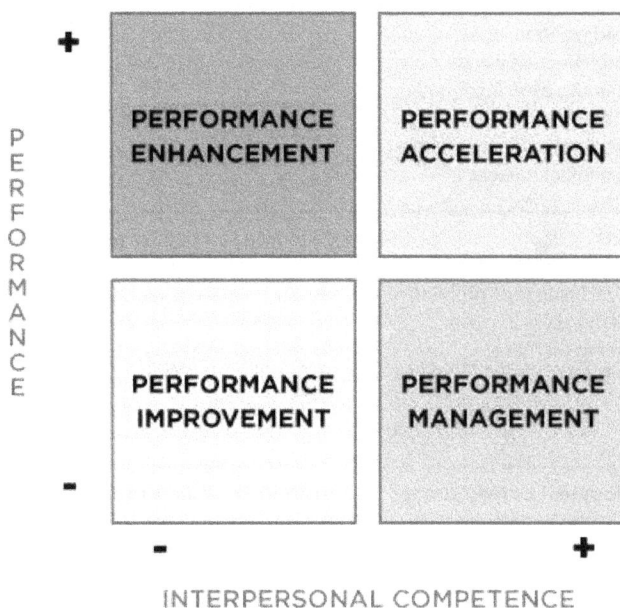

The Envisia Leaning, Inc., *Performance Coaching Model* is based on two important factors: 1) Overall job performance and 2) Interpersonal competence. Figure 4-7 provides a typology of four coaching approaches, each targeting specific goals and methods aimed at facilitating both "what gets done" (performance) and "how things get done" (social competence) for all employees within an organization. A manager or coach can use this model to quickly identify the best coaching approach to facilitate the development of talent at all levels.

Performance Enhancement Coaching (High Performance/ Low Interpersonal Competence)

- Employees at all levels who demonstrate generally high job performance but are characterized as less likable or interpersonally competent can best be helped by utilizing a _Performance Enhancement_ model of coaching.
- These employees are at risk for potential "derailment" at some point in their career and might be described as "competent" but "difficult" to deal with. As a result, others may find collaborating and interacting with these individuals challenging and attempt to avoid them when possible.
- In this model, the focus of improvement is developing social, interpersonal, and communication skills that might potentially derail the employee. Generally, consultants will utilize both personality/ style and multi-rater feedback assessments (such as a focus on emotional intelligence) to help illuminate the interpersonal "blind spots" of the employee.
- Most coaching assignments will require a lengthier intervention to ensure that these employees fully understand how they are experienced and perceived by others and the potentially negative impact of their leadership, communication skills, and interpersonal style. Such employees are expected to be somewhat defensive and challenging as they sometimes lack the "self-awareness" or self-insight characterized by relatively low emotional intelligence. A great source of resources for additional information about emotional intelligence is the Consortium for

Research on Emotional Intelligence in Organizations at www. eiconsortium.org

Performance Enhancement Developmental Strategies:

- Provide direct and candid feedback, asking for what you want the person to do more, less, or differently particularly in the interpersonal area
- Consider utilizing coaching to avoid derailment
- Utilize a 360-degree feedback process and development plan, focusing on enhancing interpersonal competence
- Measure and monitor team, department, and staff engagement
- Introduce and utilize a "balanced scorecard" to emphasize both task and interpersonal factors associated with performance

Performance Improvement Coaching (Low Performance/ Low Interpersonal Competence)

- Employees at all levels who demonstrate generally low job performance and also could be characterized as less likable or interpersonally difficult, can best be helped by utilizing a *Performance Improvement* model of coaching. These employees are sometimes offered coaching as a last resort before outplacement by many organizations. The use of outside coaching services should be questioned, as these low performers typically show little return on investment for such interventions.
- Consultants approached by companies asking for help with such employees should carefully contract with the employee system to clarify potential issues around assessment, confidentiality, and the role of human resources in the coaching intervention. Often, organizations believe that offering coaching services to these chronically poor performers will help minimize any possible wrongful termination lawsuit that could develop.

- This is another reason consultants should carefully structure the intervention if they decide to proceed with this type of employee. It is easy for consultants to feel pressured by these employees' managers or even by human resources, for a candid evaluation about the suitability or "fit" of the employee. Make sure that as a coach you don't become a natural part of the progressive discipline process by simultaneously playing an evaluation and coaching role within the employee system and with the employee, respectively. Too many non-experienced (and experienced) consultants have been tempted by these types of requests for help by an organization, only to realize too late that the hidden agenda was not to truly help the employee but to gather additional information confirming that the employee was a poor fit.
- In this particular coaching model, the focus is on the immediate and significant performance improvement of the employee. These employees are often in the low-performing 10 percent that many companies look to eliminate by offering specific outplacement and severance packages. Such poorly performing and low-potential employees can cripple morale, interfere with team functioning, and take tremendous management time away from high performers. Consultants who work with such employees typically have concrete and specific developmental action plans to support the efforts of management to "turn these employees around" and enhance current performance.

Performance Improvement Developmental Strategies:

- Diagnose if the performance deficit is due to lack of knowledge, skills, or motivation
- Seek human resources consultation about documentation and your progressive discipline process

- Set concrete performance goals and expectations
- Follow up to ensure performance improvement targets are met
- Reinforce and reward desired behaviors

Performance Acceleration Coaching (High Performance/ High Interpersonal Competence)

- Employees at all levels demonstrating a high level of performance and demonstrating interpersonal competence can further be developed by utilizing a *Performance Acceleration* model of coaching. These high-potential employees are the "lovable stars" that organizations want to retain over time.
- In this model, the focus is on leveraging the strengths of these employees and enhancing their "star" potential. Generally, consultants will utilize diverse approaches for assessment, including targeted interviews with critical stakeholders, personality/style tools, and skill-based multi-rater feedback instruments.
- These employees are expected to be fairly responsive, open, and eager to learn, making the coaching engagement typically easier. As such, they will be looking for greater specificity in feedback and targeted resources to facilitate their development. Such employees will tend to keep consultants challenged, because they are motivated, as well as interested in learning as much as possible to leverage what they do well and become even better.

Performance Acceleration Developmental Strategies:

- Carry an assignment from beginning to end
- Become involved in a merger, acquisition, strategic alliance, or partnership opportunity
- Implement an organization-wide change initiative
- Negotiate agreements with external organizations

- Operate in a high-pressure or high-visibility situation
- Head a visible committee or organization-wide task force
- Look for relevant volunteer opportunities outside of the organization.
- Engineer "stretch assignments" and developmental activities
- Consider using an executive coach to enhance "signature strengths"
- Encourage work-life balance
- Champion future career potential with other senior managers
- Structure a mentoring relationship

Performance Management Coaching (Low Performance/ High Interpersonal Competence)

- Employees at all levels who demonstrate one or more deficiencies in specific competency areas (e.g., planning, oral presentation, writing, delegation, time management) but are seen as basically collaborative and likable can best be developed by utilizing a *Performance Management* model of coaching. These employees are highly responsive to coaching specifically geared toward facilitating key competencies and skill areas that might be preventing high performance.
- In this model, the focus of improvement is in developing specific techniques, skills, and abilities. Consultants might utilize more interactive approaches to model behavior, video tape employees in action, and use employee simulations to help facilitate learning. Most coaching assignments will be task-focused and shorter in duration, based on a demonstration of skill acquisition by the employee to key stakeholders within the organization. Such employees will typically have high emotional intelligence and respond to specific instruction and more pragmatic techniques and tools.

Performance Management Developmental Strategies:

- Use skill-based training programs (internal or external)
- Utilize strategic developmental experiences to enhance specific competencies related to performance
- Model desired behavior, provide instruction, support skills practice, and reinforce desired behaviors
- Consider short-term, skill-based coaching

Evaluating Performance Coaching Interventions

It is important to think about metrics and approaches to evaluating coaching at the beginning of the intervention. Each of the four performance coaching models should be evaluated based upon the specific, agreed upon goals of the intervention. Figure 4-10 shows a comparison of the four performance coaching approaches and ways to evaluate them. Some of the following should be considered as part of an overall "performance coaching evaluation scorecard:"

- Analyze a change in scores before and after 360-degree feedback assessment (12 to 24 months following the first administration).
- Analyze the progress made on the employee's professional development plan (e.g, periodic goal evaluation or "progress pulse").
- Analyze "post-then" change scores from the employee on self-perceived changes in knowledge, skills, and behavior. This is the comparison of self-ratings before the intervention began, which is known as the "then" perspective, to those after the coaching intervention is done, which is known as the "post" perspective.
- Analyze post-coaching progress viewed by key stakeholders within the employee system (e.g., the employee's manager, internal and external customers, colleagues, etc.).

Figure 4-8

Envisia Learning Performance Coaching Comparisons

Type of Coaching	Focus	Duration	Coaching Effectiveness	Typical Metrics
Performance Improvement	Enhance Current Performance	1-3 months	Very Low	Performance Improvement Measures Performance Reviews Grievances/ Complaints
Performance Acceleration	Enhance Strengths	3-12 months	Very High	Staff/ Customer Satisfaction Promotion/ Succession Employee Engagement
Performance Enhancement	Enhance Interpersonal Deficits	3-12 months	Low	Emotional Intelligence Employee Engagement Retention/ Turnover Grievances/ Complaints
Performance Management	Enhance Task Management Performance	1-3 months	High	Skills Assessment and Improvement

Summary

As reviewed throughout the *Enable* section, it is imperative for consultants to approach every stage of an employee's learning with carefulness and detail. When designing goals, consultants and employees should collaborate to identify goals that are appropriate. Using the goal-setting tips such as *Practice Plans* and *Goal Mentors* can help translate intentions into deliberate practice which underlies all successful long-term behavior change efforts. In addition, providing knowledge and expectations about the process of learning new behaviors can help employees through their journey. In particular, consultants should view slips and setbacks as a part of the learning process, so that high-learning goals will repeatedly be set. If failures are judged severely, less difficult or vague and abstract goals are likely to become the norm (Latham & Locke, 2006).

Various measurement tools can be useful resources to track employee progress. When employee goals are not achieved, it is time to assess the reasons why. For example, consultants need to gauge their employees' "set points" around their abilities. Perhaps a goal that was perceived as attainable during its creation was soon realized as "unattainable" when practiced. Under these circumstances, the goals may need to be altered to fit the employee's set points of ability.

Managers and consultants can employ the Envisia Learning Performance Coaching model as a way to target specific developmental goals based on a employee's current job performance and interpersonal competence. This model offers specific approaches for enhancing specific skills and tools for talent at all levels of the organization.

Key Points

1. Intentions to change behavior aren't necessarily a good predictor of whether an individual will *actually* change behavior. Goal intentions do not always result in goal implementations.

2. Consultants can guide employees to translate goal *intentions* into *implementation* by using Practice Plans (i.e., habit triggers).

3. It's easy to "lapse" and even easier to relapse to return to our old habits. Consultants can utilize *relapse prevention* tips and strategies to help employees prepare for and cope with lapses.

4. Creating the right supportive environment at work and away from work helps to maintain deliberate practice and helps facilitate neural circuits to make the behavior automatic (*unconscious competence*).

5. Consultants can help employees develop using a variety of developmental tasks, exercises, and assignments, such as activities outside of work (e.g., volunteering), and using the Envisia Learning *Performance Coaching Model.*

6. Consultants should use frequent reminders, encourage employees to track and monitor goal progress and evaluate effectiveness to help reinforce maintenance of behavioral change efforts.

Enable References

Amabile, T. M. & Kramer, S. J. (2011). The power of small wins. *Harvard Business Review, 89*, 70-80.

Bogg, T. & Roberts, B. W. (2013). The case for conscientiousness: Evidence and implications for a personality marker of health and longevity. *Annals of Behavioral Medicine, 45*, 278-288.

Bonezzi, A., Brendl, C., & De Angelis, M. (2011). Stuck in the Middle: The Psychophysics of Goal Pursuit, *Psychological Science, 7*, doi:10.1177/0956797611404899.

Barrick, M. R., Mount, M. K. & Strauss, J. P. (1993). Conscientiousness and performance of sales representatives: Test of the mediating effects of goal setting. *Journal of Applied Psychology, 5, 715–722.*

Beck, J. W., Gregory, J. B. & Carr, A. (2009). Balancing development with day-to-day task demands: A multiple-goal setting approach to executive coaching. *Industrial and Organizational Psychology, 2*, 293-296.

Carver, C. S. & Scheier, M. F. (1998). Control theory: A useful conceptual framework for personality-social, clinical, and health psychology. *Psychological Bulletin, 92*, 111-135.

Chandon, P., Smith, R., Morowitz, V., Spangenberg, E. & Sprott, D. (2011). When does the past repeat itself? The interplay of behavior prediction and personal norms. *Journal of Consumer Behavior, 38*, 420-430.

Collins, C. & Bell, B. (2013). The State of the Aret in Peformance Management: Learnings from Discussions with Leading Organizations. *People & Strategy, 36*, 50-52.

Cooper, C.L. & Barling, J. (Eds.), (2008), Sage Handbook of Organizational Behavior. 1, (234-261). Thousand Oaks, CA: Sage.

Culbert, S. & Rout, L. (2010). *Get rid of the performance review*. New York: Business Plus.

DeShon R. P. & Gillespie, J. Z. (2005). A motivated action theory account of goal orientation. *Journal of Applied Psychology, 90*, 1096 – 1127.

Duckworth, A. L., Peterson, C., Matthews, M. D. & Kelly, D. R. (2007). Grit: Perseverance and passion for long-term goals. *Personality Processes and Individual Differences, 92*, 1087.

Dweck, C. S. & Leggett, E. L. (1988). A social-cognitive approach to motivation and personality. *Psychological Review, 95*, 256-273.

Elliot, E. S. & Dweck, C. S. (1988). Goals: An approach to motivation and achievement. *Journal of Personality and Social Psychology, 54*, 5-12.

Erez, A. & Judge, T. A. (2001). Relationship of core self-evaluations to goal setting, motivation, and performance. *Journal of Applied Psychology, 86,* 1270-1279.

Ericsson, K. A. (2006). *The influence of experience and deliberate practice on the development of superior expert performance.* In Ericsson, K. A., Charness, N., Feltovich, P. & Hoffman, R.R. (Eds.), Cambridge Handbook of Expertise and

Expert Performance, 683-703. Cambridge, UK: Cambridge University Press. Ericsson, K. A. (1996). *The acquisition of expert performance: An introduction to some of the issues.* In K. A. Ericsson (Ed.). The road to excellence: The acquisition of expert performance in the arts and sciences, sports, and games, 1-50.

Fung, C., Woods, J., Asch, S., Glassman, P. & Doebbeling, B. (2004). Variation in implementation use of computerized clinical reminders in an integrated healthcare system. *The American Journal of Managed Care, 10*, 878-885.

Gollwitzer, P. M., & Sheeran, P. (2006). Implementation intentions and goal achievement: A meta-analysis of effects and processes. *Advances in Experimental Social Psychology, 38*, 69-119.

Hagger, M. S., Wood, C., Stiff, C., & Chatziarantis, N. L. D. (2010). Ego depletion and the strength model of self-control: A meta-analysis. *Psychological Bulletin, 136*, 495-525.

Hofmann, W., Vohs, K.D., & Baumeister, R. F. (2012). What people desire, feel conflicted about, and try to resist in everyday life. *Psychological Sciences, 23*, 582-588.

Hölzel, B., Carmody, J., Vangel, M., Congleton, C., Yerramsetti, S., Gard, T. & Lazar, S.W. (2011). Mindfulness practice leads to increases in regional brain gray matter density. Psychiatry Research. *Neuroimaging, 191*, 36-43.

Ilies, R., Gerhardt, M. W., & Le, H. (2004). Individual differences in leadership emergence: Integrating meta-analytic findings and behavioral genetics estimates. *International Journal of Selection and Assessment, 12*, 207–219.

Judge, T., Locke, E. & Durham, C. (1997). The dispositional causes of job satisfaction. A core evaluations approach. *Journal of Applied Psychology, 83*, 17-34.

Judge, T. & Ilies, R. (2002). Relationship of Personality to Performance Motivation: A Meta-Analytic Review. *Journal of Applied Psychology, 87*, 797–807.

Koo, M. & Fishback, A. (2010). Climbing the goal ladder: How upcoming actions increase the level of aspiration. *Journal of Personality and Social Psychology, 99*, 1-13.

Lally, P. (2010). How are habits formed: Modeling habit formation in the real world. *European Journal of Social Psychology, 40*, 998–1009.

Lally, P., van Jaarsveld, C. H. M., Potts, H. W. W., & Wardle, J. (2010). How are habits formed: Modeling habit formation in the real world. *European Journal of Social Psychology, 40*, 998-1009.

Larimer, M. E., Palmer, R. S. & Marlatt, G. A. (1999). An Overview of Marlatt's Cognitive Behavioral Model. *Alcohol Research & Health, 23*, 151-160.

Latham, G. P. (2003). A five-step approach to behavior change. *Organizational Dynamics, 32*, 309-318.

Lawton, R., Conner, M., & McEachan, R. (2009). Desire or reason: Predicting health behaviors from affective and cognitive attitudes. *Health Psychology, 28*, 56–65.

Linde, J. A., Jeffrey, R.W., Finch, E.A., Ng, D. M., & Rothman, A.J. (2004). Are unrealistic weight loss goals associated with outcomes for overweight women? *Obesity Research, 12*, 569-576.

Locke, E.A. & Latham, G.P. (1990). *A theory of goal setting and task performance.* Englewood Cliffs, NJ: Prentice Hall.

Locke, E. A. & Latham, G. P. (2002). Building a practically useful theory of goal setting and task motivation. A 35-year odyssey. *The American Psychologist, 57,* 705-717.

Lombardo, M. M. & Eichinger, R. W. (1989). *Eighty Eight Assignments for Development in Place.* Center for Creative Leadership.

McGowen, K. (2010). The New Quitter: Falling Off the Wagon-Whether by Bakery Binge or Drug Bender-Doesn't Mean Total Defeat. *Psychology Today, 43,* 78-84.

Miller, G. & Wrosch, C. (2007). You've Gotta Know When to Fold 'Em: Goal Disengagement and Systemic Inflammation in Adolescence. *Psychological Science, 18,* 773-777.

Mitchell, T. R., Thompson, K. R. & George-Falvy, J. (2000). *Goal setting: Theory and practice.* In C. L. Cooper & E. A. Locke (Eds.), Industrial and organizational psychology: Linking theory with practice (pp. 216– 249). New York: Wiley- Blackwell.

Murphy, M. (2012). *Leadership IQ Study: Are SMART Goals Dumb?* Washington, DC, Leadership IQ.

Nauert, R. (2011) Brain Structure Changes after Meditation. Retrieved January 24,2011, from http://psychcentral.com/news/2011/01/24/brain-structure-changes-aftermeditation/22859.html.

Neal, D., Wood, W. & Drolet, A. (2013). How do people adhere to goals when willpower is low? The profits (and pitfalls) of strong habits. *Journal of Personality and Social Psychology, 104,* 959-975.

Norcross, J., Mrykalo, S., & Blagys, M. (2002). Auld Lang Syne: Success predictors,change processes, and self-reported outcomes of New Year's resolvers and non- resolvers. *Journal of Clinical Psychology, 58,* 397-405.

Nowack, K. M. (2016). Toxic Bosses May Cause Health Risk. Talent Management Magazine, 12, pp.26-29, 5.

Nowack, K. M. (2015). Urban Talent Myths Exposed. *Talent Management Magazine.* 11, 35-37, 4.

Nowack, K. M. (2015). The Myths and Limits of Deliberatge Practice. *Talent Management Magazine.* 11, 22-25.

Nowack, K. & Mashihi, S. (2012). Evidence Based Answers to 15 Questions about Leveraging 360-Degree Feedback. *Consulting Psychology Journal: Practice and Research, 64,* 3, 157–182.

Rhodes, R. E. & Smith, N .E. (2006). Personality correlates of physical activity: a review and meta-analysis. *British Journal of Sports Medicine, 40,* 958-965.

Rhodes, R. E., Plotnikoff, R. C., & Courneya, K. S. (2008). Predicting the physical activity intention-behavior. *Annals of Behavioral Medicine, 36,* 244–252.

Pascual-Leone, A., Amedi, A., Fregni, F. & Lotfi, B. (2005). The Plastic Human Brain Cortex. *Annual Review of Neuroscience, 28,* 377-401.

Pascual-Leone, A., D. Nguyet, L.G. Cohen, et al. 1995. Modulation of muscle responses evoked by transcranial magnetic stimulation during the acquisition ofnew fine motor skills. *Journal of Neurophysiology. 74,* 1037–1045.

Pelletier, L. G., Dion, S. C., Slovinec-D'Angelo, M. & Reid, R. (2004). Why do you regulate what you eat? Relationships between food regulation, eating behaviors, sustained dietary change and psychological adjustment. *Motivation and Emotion, 28,* 250-260.

Peterson, S., Luthans, F., Avolio, B., Walumbwa, F. & Zhang, Z. (2011) Psychological capital and employee performance: A latent growth modeling approach. *Personnel Psychology, 64,* 427-450.

Pope, D. & Simonsohn, U. (2011). Round numbers as goals. Evidence from baseball, SAT takers, and the lab. *Psychological Science, 22,* 71-79.

Schmidt, A. M. & Deshon R. P. (2010). The moderating effects of performance ambiguity on the relationship between self-efficacy and performance. *The Journal of Applied Psychology, 95*, 572-81.

Schmidt, A. M. & DeShon, R. P. (2007). What to do? The effects of goal-performance discrepancies, superordinate goals, and time on dynamic goal prioritization. *Journal of Applied Psychology, 92*, 928-941.

Schunk, D. H. (2001). *Self-regulation through goal setting.* ERIC/CLASS Digest, 1-6,Retrieved January 24, 2011, from http://www. eric.ed.gov/PDFS/ ED462671.pdf.

Shilts, M. K., Horowitz, M. & Townsend, M. S. (2004). Goal setting as a strategy for dietary and physical activity behavior change: A review of the literature. *American Journal of Health Promotion, 19*, 81-93.

Tartaglia, E. M., Bamert, L., Mast, F. W. & Herzog, M. H. (2009). Human Perceptual Learning by Mental Imagery. *Current Biology, 19*, 2081-2085.

Webb, Thomas L. & Sheeran, P. (2006). Does changing behavioral intentions engender behavior change? *Psychological Bulletin, 132*, 249-268.

Wegner, D. M. (2009). How to think, say, or do the precisely the worst thing for any occasion. *Science, 325,* 48-50.

Wood, W. & Neal, D. (2007). A new look at habits and habit goal interface. *Psychological Review, 114*, 843-863.

Wrosch, C., Miller, G. E., Scheier, M. F., & Brun de Pontet, S. (2007). Giving up on unattainable goals: Benefits for health? *Personality and Social Psychology Bulletin, 33*, 251-265.

ABOUT THE AUTHOR

Kenneth Nowack, Ph.D.

Dr, Kenneth M. Nowack is a licensed psychologist (PSY 13758) and President & Chief Research Officer of Envisia Learning (www. envisialearning.com) and Ofactor (www.ofactor.com). Ken has over 20 years of experience in the development and validation of human resource systems, assessment tools, organizational climate surveys, questionnaires, simulations, and tests

Ken has conducted research and published extensively in the areas of 360-degree feedback systems, health psychology, survey research, training evaluation, assessment, and personnel testing. He has also authored numerous assessment instruments and learning systems.

He received his B.S. and M.S. degrees in Educational Psychology at the University of California, Davis, and his Ph.D. in Counseling Psychology from UCLA. He serves as a member of the Consortium for Research on Emotional Intelligence in Organizations (www.eiconsortium.org) and is the Associate Editor for the *Consulting Psychology Journal: Research and Practice.*

www.ingramcontent.com/pod-product-compliance
Lightning Source LLC
Chambersburg PA
CBHW071630200326
41519CB00012BA/2232